Financial Planning
for **Families** of the
Fallen

Preserving Their Legacy

2018 Edition

Eric C. Jackson, CPA/PFS, CFP®, ChFC®

To all the brave men and women who have served our country, and to all the loved ones they have left behind

Introduction

Thank you for your loved one's service and sacrifice to our country, and for the sacrifices that you and your family continue to make. I consider it an honor to be able to assist you in any way.

My greatest desire is to help alleviate some of the weight or stress of the financial responsibilities that have been placed upon you, and to honor your fallen Service Member's legacy. I hope to help you to make wise decisions on important financial matters that can have a significant impact on you and your family in the near and long-term future, especially if you feel overwhelmed by the amount of information that you receive or by the important decisions that you are required to make (often on short notice).

In addition, I hope to help minimize the pressure that other people put on you to make decisions that you may not feel completely comfortable with or that you do not fully understand.

Intended Reader

I am speaking directly to you if you are a Surviving family member of a Fallen Military Service Member, and more specifically if you are a recipient or beneficiary of any financial support.

I acknowledge that those in a support role may benefit from reading this book, although it is not specifically addressed to them.

Many benefits apply differently depending on whether you are a surviving spouse, parent, child or other beneficiary, so I address each topic accordingly and with appropriate headings. It is not necessary, therefore, for you to read this book from cover to cover – you may safely skip parts that do not apply to you. The first section, however, addresses important general planning topics that I hope will be useful to all.

Background

I became a financial counselor to Military Survivors through the Army Survivor Outreach Services (SOS) program in April of 2009, and the first advice I was given was that I should counsel you to delay making any financial decisions for at least six months after the loss of a loved one. However, I quickly learned that everyone is different, everyone's circumstances and situations are unique, and a six-month delay in decision making is often impossible due to the pressure that people immediately place upon you to make important and sometimes lasting financial decisions.

Some laws and benefits require you to act within a limited amount of time or lose out entirely. Other decisions may be unavoidable or difficult to delay, or may result in unfortunate and potentially irreversible consequences if handled incorrectly.

So although you may want to avoid making most decisions, or to simply "get them over with" by doing what other people tell you to do, I want you to know that there are people available who care, who are knowledgeable and who are willing to help you in every possible way. I would love to ensure that you have the best information and resources available so that you can do your very best with what you have to work with. You should never have to feel alone or totally uncertain about the choices that you make as you move forward through this difficult process.

Through my continued work as a beneficiary financial counselor via the VA sponsored FinancialPoint® program since 2011, I have provided full-scale financial planning services to Military Life Insurance Beneficiaries from all branches of service. In so doing, I have learned that your needs and your situation are unique and constantly changing, and you therefore need customized and ongoing guidance with the flexibility to make changes as needed. Some issues can become very complex and may require the assistance of multiple people/professionals to help you to make the best decisions possible.

I love this work. I love working with you special families. I hope that I can make a positive difference to you in a meaningful way.

2018 Edition

This is the second edition and contains updates to reflect current benefit amounts and several recent law changes that have affected various benefits and programs. I also improved the clarity and detail of the verbiage in several sections.

I want this book to be useful to you and to reflect your actual and current needs, so I like to include up-to-date data regarding benefit amounts and program details. I know that many things change each year and I realize that this work is never finished.

I hope that you will provide me with feedback to improve the book, and request of me additional topics to be addressed in future editions. I intend to continue to update this book each year as laws and programs and benefits change, and as I receive your feedback. I of course welcome your comments so that together we can improve this work and ensure that it contains the best and most current information that you need and want.

I hope that more and more Surviving Family members and service providers learn and know the important topics covered in this book. I hope to ensure that good, consistent, accurate, easy to understand information and advice about benefits and other financial topics for Military Surviving Family Members will soon be relied upon consistently worldwide.

I have launched a website to support the book and mission of helping you with your finances and benefits. I know that many things change too often to wait for an annual update. So please visit www.militarysurvivor.com for the most up to date and current information, and to provide me with valuable feedback and suggestions. You can also call my office at 719-313-5815 or email me at eric@militarysurvivor.com.

Disclaimers

(Lawyer/etc. talk:)

The information contained within this book is strictly for educational purposes. If you wish to apply ideas contained in this book, you take full responsibility for your actions.

Information contained herein is not personal financial, legal or accounting advice and should not be construed as such. This book is not intended to be a substitute for the financial, legal or accounting advice of a licensed professional. You should consult with an attorney, accountant or financial advisor in any matters relating to your personal finances, accounting or legal matters.

I have made every effort to ensure the accuracy of the information within this book was correct at time of publication. I do not assume and hereby disclaim any liability to any party for any loss, damage, or disruption caused by errors or omissions, whether such errors or omissions result from accident, negligence, or any other cause.

100% of net proceeds from sales of this book will go toward Military Survivor causes

Table of Contents

Section Three: Lump Sum Benefits

Section Four: Other Benefits and Programs

Section Five: Other Financial Topics

Appendix

Acronyms

AER – Army Emergency Relief

AFAS – Air Force Aid Society

AMT – Alternative Minimum Tax

BAH – Base Allowance for Housing

CAO – Casualty Assistance Officer (Army)

CACO – Casualty Assistance Calls Officer (Navy, Marines and Coast Guard)

CAR – Casualty Assistance Representative (Air Force)

CFP® – CERTIFIED FINANCIAL PLANNER™

ChFC® – Chartered Financial Consultant®

CGMA – Coast Guard Mutual Assistance

CNO – Casualty Notification Officer

CPA – Certified Public Accountant

DEA – Dependents' Education Assistance Program

DG – Death Gratuity

DFAS – Defense Finance and Accounting Service

DIC – Dependency and Indemnity Compensation

DOD – Department of Defense

EITC – Earned Income Tax Credit

FAFSA – Free Application for Federal Student Aid

FDIC – Federal Deposit Insurance Corporation

FSGLI – Family Servicemembers Group Life Insurance

FY – Fiscal Year

HAP – Homeowner's Assistance Program

IRA – Individual Retirement Arrangement

JPPSO – Joint Personal Property Shipping Office

LOD – Line of Duty

NMCRS – Navy–Marine Corps Relief Society

OSGLI – Office of Servicemembers Group Life Insurance

SBP – Survivor Benefit Plan

SGLI – Servicemembers Group Life Insurance

SOS – Survivor Outreach Services

SSIA – Special Survivor Indemnity Allowance

TDP – Tricare Dental Program

TRDP – Tricare Retiree Dental Program

TSGLI – Servicemembers Group Life Insurance Traumatic Injury Protection

VA – Veterans Affairs

VGLI – Veterans Group Life Insurance

Section One

Preservation

"The art is not in making money, but in keeping it."

The first and most important step to permanent financial stability is to ensure that monthly income exceeds monthly expenses, and that any lump sums received remain intact. If you have recently received a significant sum of money, please do your best to not change your current habits or spending (unless they are poor habits, of course). Avoid giving money away or making major purchases or long-term commitments or investments until you can do a full assessment of your current and future financial needs, and therefore plan your spending and giving in a way that will not harm you or your family financially. Please do not rush or make any quick, hasty, or emotional financial decisions of any kind. Any money you receive may be needed to ensure your future financial stability, and should be handled with extreme care and caution.

Chapter One

Family and Friends

"There are two types of people – those who come into a room and say, 'Well, here I am,' and those who come in and say, 'Ah, there you are.'"
- Frederick Collins

Some people may give you suggestions about what you should do with money. Some may try to pressure you to make certain decisions, attempt to control you in some way, or ask you for gifts, "loans" or for an "investment" in a project or a business.

As well-meaning as they may be, some of their advice and suggestions could cause you significant harm or discomfort, financially and/or emotionally.

Family and friends or other people you know will likely react very differently when it comes to money. Their reactions may tell you something about their character that you did not previously observe. Some people may unfortunately say completely inappropriate, ignorant or insensitive things.

There may be nothing more revealing about people than how they treat you after the loss of a loved one. You may notice that your ability to discern the truth and see through facades to know if someone truly cares about you is greatly enhanced.

If you have not already, you might find yourself re-evaluating who your true friends are. Friends and family members tend to show their true colors sooner or later as they interact with you, and they can sadly be the source of great financial stress or even regret.

So when you consider their advice, I recommend that you proceed with extreme caution. Too often, I find that family and friends are the source of the greatest and quickest loss of money.

When considering whether to take the advice of a friend, family member, acquaintance, etc. first ask yourself:

Is this person extremely qualified and experienced in the area of advice that he/she is giving?

Are there any conflicts between my interests and his/hers?

Will this person benefit personally if I take the recommendation, or is the suggestion made completely out of a desire to help me?

If the person making the suggestion has your best interests at heart and is an expert in the field, the advice may be helpful. However, it would be wise to obtain a few more objective opinions from qualified individuals prior to acting on any recommendation. Also, make sure that you feel completely comfortable about your decision, and that you are confident about your level of understanding of the risks and potential negative outcomes.

"Friendship is like money, easier made than kept."
- Samuel Butler

Chapter Two

Gifts

"Let us not be satisfied with just giving money. Money is not enough, money can be got, but they need your hearts to love them. So, spread your love everywhere you go." - Mother Theresa

Gifts can be a great and meaningful part of life. However, they should be considered with great care and thoughtfulness, as their impact can be great on both the giver and the receiver, for good or for bad.

If seeing a large balance in your bank account is too frequent or painful a reminder of what has happened, consider opening a new account or transferring the money to one that you may not see very frequently, which can act as a temporary holding place. Please do not give it away before you have determined the financial and emotional impacts it may have on you and the receiver(s).

Avoid the temptation of using giving as a coping

mechanism, especially if you are feeling any guilt about money. Getting rid of all the money you receive will most likely make things worse, not better. Giving may provide some pleasure, satisfaction or relief, but it may also increase the amount of guilt that you feel as you wonder if you did the "right" or "best" thing with the money.

Questions to ask yourself prior to giving away any money:

Have I done an overall financial plan and considered all of my current and future financial needs?

If so, do I have extra money to give away?

If not, do I still feel an emotional obligation to give this gift, regardless of the financial impact it may have on me?

Would I be upset if the receiver did not use the gift as I intend?

What if I found out that my gift was squandered or immediately re-gifted to someone else? Would I regret giving the gift?

If so, how can I modify my gift to achieve the intended goal?

If I give a generous gift, how will I react if the receiver is either ungrateful or asks for more?

Is this the total gift to this person, or do I plan to give again in the future?

If I plan to give again, what circumstances will justify future giving?

Will there ever be an end to the giving? If so, what will I do to help my friend/family member transition to not needing my help in the future?

If you have not already, I highly recommend obtaining a professional, objective analysis of your overall finances so that you have a very clear, realistic evaluation of your current and future financial needs. The analysis should come from a qualified, unbiased third party with minimal/no conflicts of interest so that you can receive an objective, realistic determination of your finances. You most likely have access to this service at no cost to you if you are an SGLI beneficiary through the FinancialPoint® program, or there may also be financial counselors who can assist you in many ways regardless of your beneficiary status through Army Survivor Outreach Services, the Navy Gold Star Program, or a financial readiness program at a military installation nearest you. See chapter seven for more details.

Consider the impact of your gift on the receiver. Keep in mind that a person's habits often dictate their financial situation, so giving money may only have a temporary impact at best. If you would like your gift to make a long lasting impact in someone's life, it is important to first consider the habits and overall financial condition of the intended receiver, and then determine what would make the greatest difference to him/her. Keep in mind that if the person that you intend to help is unprepared to handle your gift (monetary or otherwise) and therefore makes unwise decisions with it, it may fill their lives (and potentially yours) with regret rather than the good that you intend.

Another problem that I have encountered with gift giving is that the receiver may believe that he/she has found in you a new source of funding whenever problems or needs come up. I find this to be especially the case (but not always) when the gift was not initially your idea, either because he/she asked for your help or simply told you about a problem or need with which you "voluntarily" decided to assist.

Some people have a pattern of seeking help from others whenever they have a problem, rather than trying to find a solution for themselves.

"Never stand begging for that which you have the power to earn."
- Miguel de Cervantes

Nearly all people need help from others at some stage of their lives, but some people give up too easily and seek help in every way and from everyone possible. It is those people who I often hear complain when people do not help them as much as they think they should, or who express jealousy when people have something that they do not. If you are giving a gift to someone with this type of attitude, it is unlikely that your gift will ever be "enough."

On the other hand, a well thought out gift that is meaningful and given with care can have a life changing impact on someone that you love, and it will likely change you too.

"Not he who has much is rich, but he who gives much."
- Erich Fromm

Receiving Gifts

You may of course often find yourself on the receiving end of gifts, so it is important as well to take into consideration what you would have someone else do in your situation as the receiver. Some well-meaning gifts may be of little or no importance to you in and of themselves, but when considered in light of the love and intent of the giver, they may be quite meaningful. Either way, try to be conscious of the thought and intent that may have gone into any gifts that are presented to you, and do not forget to try and show kindness and gratitude to the giver. If the gift does make a meaningful impact on you, be sure to let the giver know how much it meant to you. Doing so will make the gift all the more meaningful to both of you.

Conclusion

Giving and receiving gifts can be a marvelous experience and a great joy to both yourself and others, or it can be a negative and unpleasant experience for one or both parties. So be thoughtful, conscious and realistic in your expectations when giving meaningful gifts.

"To the world you may be one person, but to one person you may be the world."

- Various/unknown

Chapter Three

Loans

"Neither a borrower nor a lender be, for loan oft loses both itself and friend..." - William Shakespeare

I put loaning in a similar category to giving, because personal loans are most often the last ones to get repaid. Banks and other financial institutions go through great lengths to make sure that they are paid back, and they lend to large numbers of people in order to reduce the harm created when one person is unable to repay their loan.

You most likely do not have this luxury.

Loaning a large sum of money to one individual creates a situation in which you can be damaged greatly by a single person not paying you back.

If you are considering loaning money to a friend or

family member, I recommend that you first ask yourself these self-assessment questions:

Would I loan money to this person if he/she was not a friend/family member?

Why is he/she asking to borrow money from me instead of a financial institution?

Would a bank or credit union provide him/her with a similar loan if requested?

Am I doing this as an investment, or as a gift?

Am I interested in being a lender? Does this type of investment appeal to me? Am I expecting a significant rate of interest?"

If I am doing this as a favor, how will I feel if the borrower does not show gratitude and do his/her best to repay me?

How will I feel about this person if he/she doesn't fulfill the terms of the agreement?

What steps will I take to recover the money if it is not willingly and timely repaid?

If you can answer all of these questions to your satisfaction, and you do expect to be repaid, I highly recommend that you sign a legally binding written agreement so that there is no confusion about the terms, and that you perform a routine credit and background check before entering into the agreement (these are simple and low cost). Even if you plan to give the loan regardless of credit/background, it is important to know exactly what you are getting into.

Keep in mind that regardless of the care that you take in doing the loan correctly, the nature of your relationship with the person may change immediately, or it will especially change if the borrower ends up defaulting on your agreement. So keep in mind the effect of adding a "lender/borrower" status to your relationship prior to entering the agreement.

Human nature may also cause you to observe your new borrower's spending habits more closely, and become the judge of whether each dollar spent should have instead been repaid to you, which could harm the relationship.

If you are not concerned about being repaid, or you would be grateful if the person does repay you but not upset if he/she does not, the effect of lending money on your relationship will likely be mitigated, and the loan therefore falls into the "gift" category (at least from your vantage point - it may still make the receiver uncomfortable / negatively affect your relationship; so if it does, I suggest that you let the borrower(s) know that you are not concerned if they do not repay you).

"A bank is a place that will lend you money if you can prove that you do not need it." - Bob Hope

Chapter Four

Debt

"Compound interest is the eighth wonder of the world. He who understands it, earns it ... he who doesn't ... pays it."
- Albert Einstein

If your loved one left behind any unpaid debts, or if you personally have some of your own that you would like to eliminate, I urge you to be careful about paying them off completely until you have reviewed your overall finances and also have a clear understanding of whether or not you are legally obligated to pay each debt. Even if you are obligated, you may have other options that may be beneficial to you. Many debts, particularly those that are not in your name and even sometimes a portion of joint debts (depending on community property laws, state laws, etc.) may become legally non-collectable at the time of death. That fact may not stop debt collectors from trying to convince you to pay debts that you are not legally responsible to pay. So be careful, and consider consulting an attorney before paying large debts.

Some debts, such as mortgages and car loans, which are secured by underlying assets, must still be paid if you wish to keep the asset. I have had some clients return vehicles to lenders, or walk away from houses that they were not interested in keeping when the loan was only in their Service Member's name (and they were not residents of community-property states), as they had no further liability regarding the debts. These were all cases in which the car or house was worth less than the balance of the attached loan, and little to no sentimental value existed. If you are considering a decision of this nature, I always recommend that you proceed with caution and obtain legal and tax advice to be sure that the decision will not have any financial or other repercussions in your specific instance. Of course, consideration should be given for any emotional attachment to the house/vehicle/etc. which may outweigh the financial aspects of the decision.

If you personally have old debts that you wish to resolve, and/or which may be affecting your credit worthiness, it is also important to determine the statute of limitations on the debt (whether enough time has passed to make the debt legally unenforceable), whether a judgement / lien has been obtained, and whether a settlement or other arrangement with creditors may be reached which may ultimately be in your best interests. There are often many options to consider with regard to resolving debts, so take caution and avoid making hasty or rash decisions.

Alert Credit Reporting Agencies

The Social Security Administration generally alerts credit reporting agencies of the death of a loved one, as do individual creditors. You may also mail each agency a copy of a death certificate: Experian – P.O. Box 4500, Allen, TX 75013; TransUnion – P.O. Box 2000, Chester, PA 19016; Equifax – P.O. Box 740256, Atlanta, GA 30374.

Identity Theft and Credit Monitoring

Identity theft has unfortunately grown as one of the greatest financial crimes in the world. You most likely have or will receive notices from government or private businesses that your information has been compromised. They may offer you small settlements or free credit monitoring services or insurance.

I generally recommend that you do all that you can to monitor and protect your identity and credit, including taking advantage of free identity theft protection coverage after data breaches, or purchasing it on your own. At a minimum, you can sign up for free credit monitoring via creditkarma.com or creditsesame.com. You should also constantly strive to protect your sensitive documents and data, and properly destroy them when no longer needed.

Credit Scores

Credit is one of the most heavily marketed "products" of the 21st century, and is therefore fairly quick and easy to fix (with some exceptions) if you are current with your debts.

In general, you can obtain a very good credit score by simply maintaining one or two revolving lines of credit (typically credit cards) with a low balance (under 30% for good scores; under 10% for the best scores). Even past settlements, judgements, foreclosures, etc. will not hold your credit score down for long once you become current on all debts and maintain a credit card with a low balance.

Timely paid vehicle loans, mortgages and personal loans may help your score a little, but are unnecessary for most people to obtain an excellent credit score.

Almost anyone can obtain a secured credit card with a small deposit and no annual fee, if necessary (typically due to bad or no credit).

Debt versus Savings/Investments

I am often asked whether you should pay off your car loan or your mortgage or your student loans with Servicemembers Group Life Insurance (SGLI) or Death

Gratuity (DG) proceeds, or whether it is prudent to obtain a loan when purchasing a house, car or funding education, etc. when you have the cash to pay for it.

Of course, it is important to take a look at your overall financial situation – current and future income and expenses, assets and liabilities, etc. prior to making such major decisions. We should also take into consideration your experience and habits with regard to saving and investing.

Ask yourself:

Do I like saving/investing? How good am I at it?

Can I earn a guaranteed rate of return on my savings/investments that is higher than the interest rate on my mortgage/proposed mortgage/loan after taxes are considered? If so, how much higher is it? Is it enough to make it worth the extra time/energy/effort/complexity involved? How much of an impact will it make on my overall financial plan?

If not, am I considering putting my money into non-guaranteed savings/investments to potentially earn higher returns?

If so, how likely is it that I can earn more than the interest rate that I am paying/would pay on my mortgage/loan? How much more can I earn? How much of an impact will it make on my overall financial plan?

Do the investments that I am considering / already own have the potential to lose money?

If so, how will I feel during times that my investments lose money, knowing that I could have paid off my debts or avoided debt altogether?

How confident am I in my investments? How well do I understand them?

If my house or car was(is) paid off, am I confident enough in my investments that I would borrow money / take out a new mortgage/loan so that I could invest more?

If not, how is it different to invest with money that I could use to pay off debt?

If you stress about investments and/or debt, your life will most likely be better off if you have less investments and less debt because you will have two less things to worry about, and therefore greater peace of mind. It will also greatly simplify your (financial) life.

History shows that with no debt and a moderate amount of savings, individuals and businesses are able to weather almost any financial storm. Many businesses fail, and many individuals go bankrupt because of crushing debt during hard times, while those with little or no debt tend to make it okay while awaiting the return of prosperous times.

"It's easy to become wealthy...if you don't have any payments."
- Dave Ramsey

However, in order to financially benefit from paying off debt or paying cash, you must save/invest the money that you would have been paying monthly toward rent or a mortgage or a car payment or student loans. Otherwise, the money that you use to pay off debt / pay cash will be "gone." In the case of a house you will often get your money back or more when you sell it, but the interest "saved" will actually be spent. If you do not make "car loan payments" to yourself, you will not have

the money to purchase your next vehicle when the time comes, or you will have to take a serious downgrade.

Ask yourself:

If I pay cash for my house/car or if I pay off my existing mortgage/loan, do I have the self-discipline to save the money that I would have paid on the mortgage/loan to build back up my savings/investments?

Taxes and Liability Protection

Taxes and liability protection are another consideration. If you are a recipient of SGLI or DG with respect to a death from injury, in most cases you have a one time opportunity within the first year after receiving the money to contribute it to potentially tax-free growth vehicles such as Roth IRA's or Coverdell Savings Accounts (discussed in detail in chapter 12). If you instead pay off debt or pay cash for a car or house, the special opportunity to contribute to a Roth IRA or Coverdell will be lost forever.

However, never let the "tail wag the dog..." or in other words, taxes are always a consideration but should never be the *main* consideration.

Numerical Considerations

From a mathematical standpoint, if your investments/savings will earn a greater rate of return than the interest on the debt (net of taxes) you would be better off keeping/obtaining debt while maintaining your investments.

But in real life, the road to higher returns is generally paved with greater risks, and you are therefore unlikely to find an investment that guarantees a meaningfully higher rate of return than your mortgage interest rate (or student loan or car loan rate).

Non-guaranteed investments will sometimes earn less than the interest rate on your debt, or may even go through times of losing money. It is emotionally difficult and requires a great deal of faith in your investment strategy to continue to feel comfortable and confident in your decision if your investments decline while you are paying interest on debt that you could have paid off.

If you keep debt while keeping investments that would be enough to pay off your debt, it is the equivalent of borrowing money to invest. For these and other reasons, I highly recommend that you do not invest in anything that you do not understand or feel confidence in, and have a realistic understanding of the potential gains and losses that you could achieve from month to month and from year to year.

Mortgage as a rent equivalent

On the other hand, if you are confident that you will always have enough income to pay your mortgage and you consider it to be a "rent equivalent" while emotionally ignoring the debt attached to it, and also assuming you owe less money on your home than it is worth, you may not feel like you are "borrowing to invest." So a poor economy or underperforming investments in the short term may not actually cause you undue stress while paying on large debts, and you may successfully end up earning more on your investments in the long term than the interest you could have saved by paying off your mortgage.

If you cannot pay cash for a house, you will either have to pay rent or a mortgage, and sometimes a mortgage payment will be less than rent would be, and you may even qualify for an income tax deduction (if you have taxable income, and itemizing is more than your standard deduction). You also have the added advantage of the house potentially going up in value while you are living there (although the risk of decline is also yours, as many people found to be significant during the recent recession or when a local real estate market has plummeted). If you obtain a fixed rate mortgage, you also benefit from generally only nominal increases in your monthly payment over time if your property taxes and homeowners insurance rates increase. Keep in mind that as an owner you are responsible for all repairs, and if you want to move you will have to go to the trouble of selling the home or making double payments for a while or becoming a landlord.

The Psychology of Making Purchases with Debt

One major problem with financing purchases is that home and car salespeople and even financial aid officers at colleges and universities know that if you do not have to shell out the cash right now for their product, you will feel differently about the value of what you are purchasing.

You may feel like you are only spending the monthly payment while ignoring the total cost. This makes it more likely that you will overpay for vehicles, homes/home upgrades and even your degree. You may not shop around or negotiate as much as you would otherwise when buying a car or house. You may make less effort to get scholarships for your education or consider the value of your degree compared to a similar, equivalent but less expensive college, if you are paying with loans.

Summary

Debt is complicated. Is it the key to your wealth? Will it make your life better? If you are still on the fence after analyzing your overall finances and answering all the questions posed in this chapter, and assuming that you qualify to re-borrow money at the same interest rates that you currently have, I recommend that you consider paying off your debts and/or paying cash for your purchases. If you find that you do not like having no debt, or that you are unable to save the money that you should save while having no debt, you can then reverse your decision by taking out new loans.

Chapter Five

Spending

"A fool and his money are soon parted." - John Bridges

Your spending habits will determine your financial success or failure in life. They form the foundation whereon all other aspects of your finances lie. If you cannot control your spending, no amount of planning or investing or strategy can rescue you from eventual financial demise.

This truth should bring you peace in knowing that you control your financial destiny. Outside influences such as the economy, the stock market, interest rates or the government may affect you but they cannot prevent you from causing your own financial success or ruin.

Spend money. But spend it on what matters most to you. Spend it in a way that maximizes the value that you receive from it, and spend it in a way that preserves your ability to always have access to the money that you need, when you need it.

"I know of no situation where happiness and peace of mind have increased with the amassing of property beyond the reasonable wants and needs of the family." - Eldon Tanner

Money is freedom - freedom to live your best life. The lack of money forces you to do things and go places that may undermine your full potential.

I created a seven-minute activity included in the appendix to help you to think through and organize what matters most to you in an efficient and precise manner. A follow through activity adds time and monetary stipulations to make it easy to tie your most important values and relationships to your spending plan.

If you do not create and live by a financial plan, others (salespeople, businesses, friends, family and/or the government) will end up with all of your money and eventually leave you with nothing.

Do more with less. Make every dollar count.

Plan your spending according to your highest desires. Use money to make your life better in meaningful ways. Money can enhance the use of your time, provide you with memorable activities, supply you with desired comforts and conveniences, enable you to experience the joy of helping others, and help you to avoid and eliminate undesirable circumstances.

If you control your money, you will find peace as you go about your life working toward your highest purposes. You will achieve greater success with your savings and investments. You will constantly strive to find ways to do more with less. You will recognize quickly whether specific purchases or opportunities truly fit your needs. You will easily identify people who care about your best interests and avoid those who selfishly try to take advantage of you. You will find courage to stand up for yourself and the needs of your family, friends and loved ones above the profit motives of a salesperson. You will not overpay for anything.

"If there is any one thing that will bring peace and contentment into the human heart, and into the family, it is to live within our means..." - Heber Grant

Chapter Six

Attitudes and Misconceptions about Money

"...[Money] is significant only to the extent that it allows you to enjoy what is important to you. And not worrying about your finances is critical..."
- Bill Bachrach

How you feel about money will greatly determine whether it will be a source of strength or peace in your life, or a burden or stress. It is your choice.

Be grateful for everything that you receive. If you feel tempted to feel entitled to something or feel like you are owed something, choose instead to be thankful for any benefit of any kind, be it money, time, trips, gifts, etc. and you will be happier for it. Nothing is free – someone pays for it in time, money, or other resources. The government or another organization may administer certain programs, but real people do make real contributions for anything that is provided in any way.

You may not feel prepared to handle the weight of the responsibility of managing your loved one's legacy. You may find that making significant decisions regarding money is very difficult. You may feel at times that you are not interested in money or that you want to avoid it altogether. You are not alone.

If you received SGLI or other proceeds, please realize that it is intended to provide you with financial security, stability, freedom, etc. It is not taxpayer funded or "blood money" as some people refer to it, but it is an optional insurance plan that your loved one decided to participate in and pay for to care for you and help take care of you if something happened. It is not government funded, but is rather administered by Prudential through the military, and millions of Service Members pay a monthly fee to participate.

You may feel the burden of not knowing what to do with SGLI proceeds. But try to think of the money as a caring gift from your loved one, and thoughtfully consider what would be best for you to do with it. If you were not financially dependent on your Service Member, you may especially feel that you do not want or need the money received as a result of his/her passing, and you may have a hard time knowing what to do with it.

If it feels uncomfortable or unnerving to see the money in your bank account, you may need to move it to an account that you do not access often, until you are ready to do something with it.

Of course, you want to do the right thing with the money and you do not want to make mistakes, so try not to rush or feel like you need to make any urgent decisions. Try not to feel pressured by anyone that is trying to convince you to make decisions that you do not feel comfortable with or that you do not understand.

Some people have mistakenly thought that if they just go along with what someone tries to convince them to do, they can just do it and "get it over with" and that their stress about the money will be gone because the decision will be "done." But the truth is that the stress or worry does not typically go away, it just changes from, "what should I do with the money? to, "what did I just do with the money?" or, "I hope I did the right thing with the money!"

You may decide to purchase something as a "gift" from your Service Member, which can be a special moment or a meaningful time of gratitude for the money that your loved one left you. But I hope that you also take into consideration your current financial situation, and do not use it as an excuse that may end up creating future financial hardship. The memory of the gift will be much sweeter if you can look back with fond memories on the purchase, and are not struggling financially as a result.

In deciding what to do with money, you might also find yourself asking, "what would [my loved one] have me do with the money?" This can be a good or a bad thing to think about. I have on occasion worked with people who had the discussion with their Service Member prior to his/her passing about what to do with the money, or who even had a written plan. I have found that such a discussion or written plan can take a huge burden off you as the beneficiary, because it can eliminate the requirement to decide what to do with it, or the feeling of guilt if things do not turn out as hoped or desired. On the other hand, I have had people use this excuse to buy things that they could not afford, and would eventually regret.

So even if your Service Member told you what he/she wanted done with the money, if he/she left it to you directly, you were most likely given full, legal decision-making authority with the money (which is the case if you were the beneficiary). So although you can take into consideration what he/she would have wanted you to do with the money, ultimately it may not be relevant based on the current situation because you of course have current insight into your needs/expenses, and ultimately, the decision is yours.

Money will not make your life better if not controlled and used for what you care about most. If used for your life's greatest priorities, it will become important and meaningful to you, and you will see it as representing the people and things you care about most, and/or freedom to use your time as you see fit. You will use money as a tool to spend more time doing the things you love most, and spending time with people you care about, thereby helping to achieve some of your life's greatest purposes. It will be sacred and important to you, and you will use it carefully.

Chapter Seven

Financial Professionals

"...You must choose wisely your investment counselors. Be sure they merit your confidence with a proven successful investment record."
- Eldon Tanner

Depending on where you live, you may have access to in-person or phone assistance from salaried military civilian employees or contractors who perform "financial counseling" services. Military "financial counselors" give information and advice regarding benefits and programs and practical matters such as budgets, but generally do not complete full financial plans or give investment advice or maintain the licenses to do so.

If you are a recipient of SGLI, as mentioned previously, you have lifetime access to a licensed financial professional either in-person or via teleconference, at no cost to you, via the VA sponsored FinancialPoint® Beneficiary Financial Counseling Service. FinancialPoint® maintains a 24-hour call center for answering questions and provides basic financial plans and a will preparation service. It also contracts with a wide range of independent advisors who can give comprehensive financial planning and investment advice, almost all of which do not sell commission products (this is my role – see chapter 12 for further details).

Private sector "financial advisors" who work at your insurance company, bank or at a local or national financial firm, and who may also be family, friends or neighbors, will most likely approach you to offer advice.

Sadly, large insurance companies control and direct the majority of the "personal financial advisor" profession, pushing highly profitable products and services to unwary customers through "captive" agents. They strive to build your trust through relationships and then hold themselves only to a "suitability" standard, often ignoring the effect of commissions, charges, fees, quality, comparability and performance of the products and services that they recommend.

Unfortunately, most banks and credit unions operate in much the same manner. They generally hire under-credentialed advisors who travel from branch to branch to sell an array of insurance and investment products and services. Most of them follow the same low "suitability" standards as insurance company agents but with a potentially wider selection of products.

Many uniquely named or privately operated financial firms/organizations also have special agreements with insurance and/or mutual fund or other investment companies to favor their products to their clients in exchange for free rent, health insurance, retirement benefits, special payouts or kickbacks, reward trips, etc.

A smaller number of independent firms maintain neutrality from insurance companies and investment company kickbacks, and may be able to offer more unbiased advice.

An even smaller number of firms do not sell any products or earn any commissions of any kind, but instead charge strictly for their advice. A commission-free model aligns your best interests with the compensation of your advisors.

However, if advisors charge for "managing assets," you must be careful about the amount of fees they charge, and what you receive in exchange for those fees. Many "asset management" programs simply set up automated trades and do very little by way of providing value for the fees. Other programs place you in many of their own funds, or in funds that give them extra kickbacks or other compensations. So although you may pay for "asset management," it still may not be aligned with your best interests.

Also, if you hire an advisor that charges strictly based on assets under management, you may not see much by way of advice with regard to practical matters, financial planning or real life integrations. Their compensation focuses on investments and their incentive is to spend as little time as possible helping you to understand or tie your investments to your overall life plans and goals. So the value of the service may be limited or even counterproductive depending on the fees. A natural incentive also exists for them to recommend that you invest more instead of paying off debts because they are paid based on the amount of money that you invest.

Some firms that "manage assets" seek to increase their compensation by placing your money in their own proprietary investment funds or by accepting kickbacks from other mutual fund or investment companies, regardless of performance. So you must still use extreme caution even when hiring an advisor or firm under a "fee-only" model.

I battle against the majority of conflict-of-interest laden bad "advice" that you will come across, and hope that most people will soon put their trust in advisors who truly look out for their best interests.

Who Should You Trust?

If someone gives you financial advice, first ask about the person's credentials and experience. The most widely recognized credentials in the industry are the Certified Public Accountant Personal Financial Specialist (CPA/PFS), Certified Financial Planner™ (CFP®), and Chartered Financial Consultant™(ChFC®). Each of these require several years of experience and/or a college degree, in addition to comprehensive examinations and continuing education requirements.

Although total years of experience may not always indicate total years of wisdom, a certain minimum threshold of experience can prevent you from becoming a "guinea pig." You do not want to have to start over on your financial plan because your advisor went broke. Some researchers indicate that up to 90% of financial professionals do not last more than four years in the industry, so you may want to consider someone who has at least made it over that hump to increase the likelihood that they can help you for years to come.

Beyond experience and credentials, I recommend secondly that you "follow the money," or in other words, know how the person giving you advice gets paid or otherwise may benefit from your decisions or outcomes.

In most cases, the very best financial professionals have

worked hard to align their financial incentives with your financial goals. They reduce or eliminate most potential conflicts of interest, thereby mitigating the temptation to give you recommendations that may not be in your best interest. In most cases, they are also fiduciaries, legally obligated to make recommendations based on your best interests at all times.

The third and perhaps most important characteristic of a good financial advisor is that he/she takes the time to listen to you and understand your needs.

The best financial plans, the ones that actually work in real life…focus on your life, your wants, your needs, and your desires. They take into account not only your financial picture, but also your emotions, your desires and your comfort level so that you are happy and confident in your decisions. Every dollar takes on true meaning, and all savings and investment decisions reflect the important people and purposes in your life.

Financial sales-people and commission-driven non-fiduciaries often skip these ever-important steps because they hurry you to take action as soon as possible. They do not get paid until you do take action. They know that if you do not "act now" they may lose your business altogether because chances are, your relationship is not very strong with them yet and you may go elsewhere.

The more care taken to ensure your comfort with and understanding of your financial plan, the more likely you are to successfully achieve your desires. Many unforeseen obstacles will likely appear along the way, so by taking necessary precautions you can prepare for uncertainty and overcome challenges to achieve your financial goals.

"When it is obvious that goals cannot be reached, do not adjust the goals, adjust the action steps." - Confucius

In summary, you may not be able to immediately judge a potential advisor's character or abilities. But you can easily narrow your list to those who align their financial interests with yours, who have obtained a significant amount of meaningful experience and credentials, and who take the time to listen.

Section Two

Income Benefits

The Military provides eligible surviving spouses, children and dependent parents with monthly incomes to assist with regular living expenses. When combined with Social Security, many families with minor children actually experience an overall increase compared to their prior monthly income.

Chapter Eight

Line of Duty
and Service Connection

Your Service Member's "line of duty" (LOD) determination will dictate your eligibility for certain benefits and programs.

Generally speaking, active-duty Service Members are considered "in line of duty" regardless of the cause of death, with the exception of illegal or criminal activities such as accidental overdoses of controlled substances, alcohol abuse and homicide (although each situation is considered individually, so there are no automatic disqualifiers).

Suicide has always resulted in a line of duty "yes" determination to my knowledge. Army regulation 600-8-4 Appendix B Rule 10 states: "The law presumes that a mentally sound person will not commit suicide (or make a bona fide attempt to commit suicide)." Therefore, a mental disconnect has occurred in which the basic human nature of self-preservation has been overcome at the moment of suicide completion, and no person or circumstance is to blame.

National Guard or Reserves Service Members are generally considered "not in line of duty" unless their death occurred while on duty (e.g. guard/reserve weekends, including traveling to/from duty).

Each decision is made on a case by case basis and can be successfully appealed in some instances if it originally comes back negative.

It may take months or more to receive the official line of duty determination, which will delay the commencement of line-of-duty-dependent income benefits, but in most cases the likely outcome is clear, so we can plan accordingly.

Service Connection

If you are a family member of a Military Retiree, Veteran or National Guard or Reserves Service Member who died from a service-connected condition while "not in line of duty", you may be eligible for certain other benefits. If service-connected status is initially denied, you also have the ability to appeal the decision, and/or to increase your loved one's disability rating, which may result in additional benefits eligibility.

Chapter Nine

Veterans Affairs (VA) Dependency and Indemnity Compensation (DIC)

Spouses

If your spouse was determined to be "in line of duty" or "service-connected," you should be eligible to receive a monthly tax free income through the U.S. Department of Veterans Affairs, called Dependency and Indemnity Compensation (DIC). DIC is paid to you for life (unless re-marriage occurs prior to age 57, although it may be reinstated if re-marriage ends) and is the same amount for all eligible spouses regardless of rank, years of service, etc.

The current monthly DIC payment for spouses is $1,283.11 (effective with the December 31, 2017 payment). It can increase each year according to the government's determination of inflation (CPI-W as determined by the Bureau of Labor Statistics, which also affects Social Security and the Survivor Benefit Plan (SBP)). In addition, if you are housebound, you may be eligible for an extra $148.91 per month; if you are in need of aid and attendance, you may be eligible for an additional $317.87 per month.

If you are caring for your Service Member's dependent minor children (or stepchildren or other minors or permanently disabled persons listed as dependent in DEERS), your monthly amount is increased by $317.87 per month for each child until they reach age 18. Also, if you are caring for at least one eligible dependent child, you are eligible to receive an extra "transitional allowance" of $270 per month for the first two years.

Disability

If your spouse had a total, continuous, service-connected disability for at least ten years (five years if total disability occurred prior to leaving active-duty service, or one year if a former prisoner of war), you would also qualify for DIC even if the cause of death was not determined to be service-connected and you were married for at least a year (or less if you had a child together).

Children

If you are under 18 and your parent was "in line of duty" and your surviving parent is un-remarried, your parent will receive $317.87 per month (effective with the December 31, 2017 payment) to assist with your care. If you are still in high school after turning age 18, the DIC will be paid directly to you until you complete high school. If you continue to college, you can elect to receive DIC until age 23, but you must relinquish it if you use any other VA educational benefits such as DEA or Fry Scholarship (Chapters 35 and 33 respectively; see chapter 15 of this book for more details), which provide significantly greater financial benefits in most cases. If you are over age 18 and it has been determined by the VA that you were permanently disabled prior to age 18, your DIC payment eligibility extends to your lifetime.

If no surviving spouse is eligible for DIC, the VA will base your monthly payment on an alternative calculation, which varies depending on how many children are eligible under your sponsor. If you are the only eligible child you will receive $541.79 per month. The "per-child" amount decreases for each additional eligible child to a minimum of $241.85 (in the case of nine or more eligible children).

Your portion is paid on your behalf to your financial guardian (typically your legal guardian) until you are 18, and then to you directly until you become ineligible either by age or by marriage or by accepting VA educational benefits.

If you plan to continue your education after high school, please consider your overall education plan to determine the best strategy for you with regard to DIC. For example, if you intend to obtain a Master's, Doctorate, Law, Medical or other post-graduate degree and will therefore attend college for more than four or five years, it may make sense to delay your acceptance of the Fry or DEA depending on your total eligibility. You can elect instead to continue receiving the DIC for up to five more years while scholarships easiest to attain.

Either way, I highly recommend that if you intend to begin college in the semester after you graduate high school, that you certify your college enrollment to the VA so that your DIC income will continue during the summer before you enter college. You must also delay your application for the Fry or DEA education benefits until you actually begin attending college. Otherwise, your DIC income will stop as soon as you graduate high school or are certified to receive the Fry or DEA. This strategy could result in two to three extra months of DIC income (depending on your age and the gap between your high school graduation and your first day of college), likely close to $1,000 extra!

Parents

You are generally eligible to receive DIC if you have limited or no income, and you are a parent of a Service Member who died in the line of duty or as a result of a service-related condition. Biological, adopted, or foster parents qualify (if foster parents for at least one year prior to the Veteran's last entry into active service).

If you are the sole surviving parent, you are eligible to receive $634 per month (plus $343 if you qualify for Aid and Attendance, which is generally defined as: blind, a patient in a nursing home, or otherwise in need of regular aid and attendance) if your annual income is not over $800 (including spousal income, if applicable, but reduced by any family medical or burial expenses you incur). If your annual income is over $800 but not over $8,622, you will receive a reduced amount ranging from $626 to $5.04 per month. If your income is between $8,662 and $14,974 (if not living with a spouse, $20,128 if you are living with a spouse) you are eligible to receive $5 per month. If your income is over $14,974 (if not living with a spouse, $20,128 if you are living with a spouse) you are not be eligible to receive any benefit.

If you are one of two Surviving parents and you are not living with a spouse, you are eligible to receive $459 per month (plus $343 if you qualify for Aid and Attendance) if your annual income is not over $800 (including spousal income, if applicable, but reduced by any family medical or burial expenses you incur). If your annual income is over $800 but less than $6,475, you will receive a reduced amount ranging from $443 to $5.04 per month. If your income is between $6,475 and $14,974 you are eligible to receive $5 per month. If your income is over $14,974 you are not eligible to receive any benefit.

If you are one of two Surviving parents and you are living with a spouse or the other parent, your benefit will be $431 per month (plus $343 if you qualify for Aid and Attendance), if your annual income is not over $1,000 (including spousal income, if applicable, but reduced by any family medical or burial expenses you incur). If your annual income is over $1,000 but less than $7,188, you will receive a reduced amount ranging from $420 to $5.04 per month. If your income is between $7,188 and $20,128 you are eligible to receive $5 per month. If your income is over $20,128 you are not eligible to receive any benefit.

Contact the VA

You can reach the VA at 800-827-1000, or you can make a secure, personal inquiry about your specific benefits at iris.custhelp.com (often more convenient and traceable than a phone call), or find an in-person service location.

Chapter Ten

Survivor Benefit Plan (SBP) and Special Survivor Indemnity Allowance (SSIA)

Spouses

If your spouse was determined to be "in line of duty" or was retired and made the election, you should receive a monthly taxable income paid to you through the Defense Finance and Accounting Service (DFAS) called the Survivor Benefit Plan (SBP). SBP is essentially the Survivor portion of your spouse's military retirement plan, and like the DIC, it is a lifetime income (unless re-marriage occurs prior to age 55, although it may be reinstated if re-marriage ends). However, it is offset (reduced) by your VA DIC income, and in some cases may be reduced to zero.

The amount you are eligible to receive varies based on your spouse's pay grade and years of service, and in most active-duty cases, amounts to 41.25% of your spouse's average base pay (averaged over up to the last 36 months of pay). The 41.25% is derived from a 55% Survivor portion of a 75% payout rate based on a full-disability retirement (equivalent to a 30 years-of-service active duty retirement, which generally accrues at the rate of 2.5% per year).

For example, an active-duty Service Member with over eight years of service and a pay grade of E-6 would have a Fiscal Year (FY) 2018 base pay of $3,454. However, the last 36 months' average pay may be closer to $3,200 depending on timing of promotions, etc. A full disability retirement rate of 75% of a $3,200 base pay would amount to $2,400; but the 55% Survivor portion of that amount would reduce the SBP to $1,320 (equal to 41.25% of $3,200). After subtracting the VA DIC offset of $1,283.11, the SBP payable to you would only be $36.89.

This may seem like not much of a benefit at all in many situations, but it certainly is better to receive the tax free DIC than to receive taxable SBP. In addition, there are three possible ways to eliminate or reduce the offset and thereby receive all or part of the SBP income concurrent with the DIC: SSIA, the remarriage exemption, and the child-only SBP option.

Special Survivor Indemnity Allowance (SSIA)

The Special Survivor Indemnity Allowance (SSIA) is a

taxable monthly income payable by DFAS to all SBP-eligible surviving spouses who are subject to the SBP-DIC offset, and is designed specifically to reduce the offset. SSIA began at $50 per month in 2009 and has gradually increased to the current $310 per month. It was scheduled to terminate on September 30, 2017, but a six-month extension has been authorized by Congress (making May 1, 2018 the last payment).

Numerous organizations are working to influence Congress to either extend or increase the SSIA or to eliminate the SBP-DIC offset altogether. Based on my observation of past congressional behavior, it would not surprise me if they wait until the day before SSIA benefits expire (or after the fact) to decide whether to extend the benefit or eliminate the offset altogether. My opinion is that Congress will most likely extend the SSIA, and perhaps make it permanent or adjusted with inflation. But of course, we will not know until it actually happens.

The remarriage exemption

The SBP-DIC offset is eliminated, strange as it may seem, if you remarry after age 57. If you get un-remarried after age 57, the offset returns. So, while married after age 57, you would receive both DIC and SBP. [Note: if you remarry between the ages of 55 and 57, your DIC eligibility would end, also eliminating the offset. Your taxable SBP income would replace most or all of the tax-free DIC, but you would also lose your SSIA income.]

This rule became effective in 2009 when in response to litigation from several widows, a court interpreted verbiage from a 2003 law that restored DIC to widows who remarry after age 57, as preventing DFAS from applying the offset to SBP. So effectively, a financial incentive now exists to remarry after age 57. Whether Congress intended this or not, I am sure that you will not complain if it ever applies to your situation.

The Child-Only SBP Option

If you are caring for your spouse's dependent child/children/stepchildren, you have the option to forego the SBP income personally so that the children may receive it until age 18 or 22 if in school (or indefinitely if permanently disabled prior to age 18 or 22 if in school). The child-only option effectively eliminates the DIC offset while the children are eligible, although it eliminates your lifetime eligibility for SBP and SSIA. If you elect to keep the SBP (Spouse-child option) either because your children are older or you want to rely on some additional lifetime income, it will automatically convert to the child-only option if you lose your eligibility for SBP (e.g. remarriage, death, etc.).

When selecting the child-only option, the total SBP eligibility will be split amongst all eligible children of your spouse (living with you or not), and will redistribute to all remaining eligible children each time any of the children becomes ineligible for benefits (e.g. by turning age 18 and not attending school or by turning age 22 if in school (or failure to submit a required education certification form while in school).

If you are the financial guardian of any or all of your spouse's minor dependent children, their SBP portion may be direct-deposited into your bank account to assist in caring for them. So your overall household income should be higher than the spouse-child option while the children are eligible. Upon turning 18 and certifying their education status, children are required to fill out a new direct deposit form to receive the income directly.

Reporting

You will be asked via an annual letter to report whether your children have married during the year, regardless of their age. Do not ignore this letter as their income will be "frozen" if you do not respond. If six months passes, you will be required to re-certify their identity at a police or military installation, which can be a great inconvenience. All "frozen" funds will be released upon re-certification, which may cause significant negative tax consequences.

Taxation

SBP is taxable income and will be reported to you on form 1099-R from DFAS. Depending on your overall situation, you may or may not owe taxes on the income. If you are taxed Federally on the income, some states such as Colorado grant an exemption from state income taxes up to a certain threshold.

If you would like to have taxes withheld or change your withholding election, you will need to fill out and send form W-4P to DFAS and choose the proper exemptions and/or extra withholding.

Children receiving SBP will also receive a 1099-R from DFAS and must report the income on their own individual tax return (if their income is high enough to trigger a filing requirement). Your child(ren) are considered dependents for income tax purposes only if their income (net of any money saved for them) is less than half the cost of supporting them.

If you are claiming a child as a dependent, Federal income taxes will be owed on any amounts over $1,050. If you are not claiming your children as dependents, they will only owe taxes on income over $7,500 ($7,650 in 2018). They will qualify for the standard deduction and personal exemption of $10,400 for 2017 (increasing to $10,650 in 2018). However, any unearned income that exceeds $7,500 (increasing to $7,650 in

2018) will be subject to Alternative Minimum Tax (AMT) of 26% (if the total tax using the Federal Income tax calculation is less than that amount). This can be reduced by charitable donations made in their name and sometimes medical bills, and claiming itemized deductions in lieu of the standard deduction.

If your total taxable income is below $10,400 ($10,650 for 2018), or if your dependent children have taxable income below $1,050, or if your non-dependent children have taxable income below $7,500 ($7,650 in 2018), you are most likely not required to file a Federal income tax return. However, if you had income tax withheld from SBP or other sources, or if you had income from working, it will be necessary to file a tax return to obtain a refund of withholdings or other tax credits.

Even if you cannot claim your children as dependents for income tax purposes, you may be able to still claim them to qualify for the Earned Income Tax Credit if you are working and meet the other requirements for the credit (e.g. having less than $3,450 in countable investment income in 2017 (increases to $3,500 in 2018)).

Corrections/Election Changes

If you were not aware of your options or you feel that you made wrong choices based on misinformation or the lack of proper information, you may request to change your election. I have worked with a number of families who were entitled to SBP income, but because of paperwork mishandling or for other reasons they were not receiving it at all. Others were unaware of the child-only option, and upon analysis of the benefit differences, realized that they could receive much more income and tens of thousands of dollars in back pay to support their family by switching to the child-only option.

Most corrections or changes need to be made within six years of becoming eligible for benefits, to go through the standard process of submitting an application. If more than six years have passed, an appeal generally must be made to the Board of Correction of Military Records, which can be a lengthy process (typically at least nine months). But many families have had success obtaining the desired adjustments, thus making it well worth their time and effort.

Children

If your parent was determined to be "in line of duty" and had no surviving spouse, or if the surviving spouse is not living or has remarried or made the child-only election, you should be eligible to receive a monthly taxable income through the Defense Finance and Accounting Service (DFAS) called the Survivor Benefit Plan (SBP). SBP is essentially the Survivor portion of your parent's military retirement plan, and like the

DIC, is paid to you until age 18 or 22 if you are in school, or indefinitely if you are disabled prior to age 18 or 22 if in school.

The amount you are eligible to receive varies based on your parent's pay grade and years of service, and in most cases amounts to 41.25% of his/her average base pay (averaged over up to the last 36 months of pay). The 41.25% is derived from a 55% Survivor portion of a 75% payout rate based on a full-disability retirement (equivalent to a 30 years-of-service active duty retirement, which generally accrues at the rate of 2.5% per year).

The total SBP eligibility will be split amongst all eligible children, and will redistribute to all remaining eligible children each time any of you becomes ineligible for benefits (e.g. by turning age 18 and not attending school or not certifying continued eligibility via required education certification forms, or turning age 22). Your surviving parent or other financial guardian will receive your SBP portion on your behalf until you are 18, after which you will be requested to submit an education certification form with direct deposit instructions so that you may receive the income directly.

Reporting

You will be asked via an annual letter to report whether you have married during the year, regardless of your age. Do not ignore this letter as your income will be "frozen" if you do not respond. If six months passes, you will be required to re-certify your identity at a police or military installation, which can be a great inconvenience. All "frozen" funds will be released upon re-certification, which may cause significant negative tax consequences.

Taxation

SBP is taxable income and will be reported to you on form 1099-R from DFAS. Depending on your overall situation, you may or may not owe taxes on the income. If you are taxed Federally on the income, some states such as Colorado grant an exemption from state income taxes up to a certain amount.

If you would like to have taxes withheld or change your withholding election, you will need to fill out and send form W-4P to DFAS and choose the proper exemptions and/or extra withholding.

If your parent/guardian claims you as a dependent, you will owe Federal income taxes on any amounts over $1,050. If you are not claimed as a dependent, you will owe taxes on income over $7,500 ($7,650 in 2018). You will qualify for the standard deduction and personal exemption of $10,400 for 2017 (increasing to $10,650 in 2018). However, any unearned income that exceeds $7,500 (increasing to $7,650 in 2018) will be subject to Alternative Minimum Tax (AMT) of 26% (if the total tax using the Federal Income tax calculation is less than that). This can be reduced by charitable donations made in your name, and sometimes medical bills, and by claiming itemized deductions instead of the standard deduction.

If your taxable income is below either of these thresholds, you may not be required to file a Federal income tax return. However, if you had income tax withheld from SBP or other sources, it will be necessary to file a tax return to obtain a refund.

Contact DFAS

You can reach DFAS at 800-321-1080 for enrollment or benefit questions or service. You can also create/manage your account at mypay.dfas.mil or request a copy of your 1099R tax form at www.dfas.mil/retiredmilitary.

Chapter Eleven

Social Security

Spouses

You should be eligible for a monthly Social Security income benefit if you are caring for your spouse's (or former spouse's) dependent children (including stepchildren, as long as they were financially dependent on your spouse for more than half of their support) while they are under the age of 16, or any age if they have been determined to be continuously disabled prior to age 22. Remarriage will end your Surviving Spouse income entitlement.

If you yourself are disabled, you are separately eligible to receive income benefits on your spouse's record if the disability began within seven years of receiving benefits for caring for your spouse's children, or at age 50 if there were no children (and your disability started within seven years of your spouse's death).

Your spouse's dependent children will also be eligible for their own separate portion of Social Security income until they reach age 18 (or up to 19 if still in High School) which will most likely be paid to you on their behalf (up until age 18) for their support and maintenance.

There is no "line of duty" requirement to receive Social Security unless you were married for less than nine months, in which case Social Security grants a special exception for active duty Service Members who receive an "in line of duty" determination.

The amount of income benefit is calculated based on each worker's pay history, so the more years worked and the higher the wages, the higher the benefit.

Family Maximum

Social Security has a "family maximum," meaning that the total combined amount paid to all family members cannot exceed a certain amount (specific to each worker). Generally speaking, the maximum is reached when there are four or more eligible beneficiaries (e.g. one spouse and three or more children, or four or more children and no spouse). When the maximum is reached, it is divided equally amongst all beneficiaries (e.g. five beneficiaries will receive the same total amount as four beneficiaries, but each person's benefit will be less). Because of this fact, if four or more of you are receiving income and one beneficiary loses eligibility, the remaining eligible beneficiaries should expect an increase in their income (it should be proportionate unless you are dropping from four to three beneficiaries, in which case it will likely only be a partial increase).

Working while receiving Social Security

If you are working and earning more than $16,920 annually (increasing to $17,040 in 2018) while eligible to receive Social Security, benefits are reduced by $1 for every $2 (50%) of any earned income that exceeds that amount.

If you have at least three children eligible to receive Social Security and you expect your portion of Social Security to be reduced because of your income from working, it may be beneficial to revoke your right to receive Social Security. Doing so should increase the amount that your children receive and eliminate the reduction that you would have because of working. Be careful not to make this decision prematurely, however, because the end result will depend on the total offset

from your actual earnings in a given year compared to the net family benefit decrease from revoking your entitlement.

Social Security Retirement

You should also be eligible for a monthly Social Security

retirement income on your spouse's record starting as early as age 60, as long as you were married for at least nine months or he/she was on active duty and determined to be "in the line of duty." If you remarry prior to age 60, you lose this entitlement (unless the remarriage ends) but become eligible to receive spousal Social Security based on your new spouse's record. If you remarry after age 60, you retain eligibility for Survivor benefits, but it must be more than your entitlement under your new spouse's record to benefit you.

If your personal Social Security entitlement from your own earnings record ends up being more than what you would receive under your spouse's record, you can switch to your own benefit as early as age 62 or as late as age 70. You cannot receive both entitlements concurrently, and you cannot switch to your spouse's record after you start using your own benefit.

Lump Sum

In most cases, Social Security pays a very small lump sum death benefit of $255, which was intended to cover burial costs when enacted in 1935 (with a cap of $315, which was reduced to $255 in 1954) but clearly comes up far short now after over 80 years of inflation. To qualify for the $255, you must have been living in the same household as your spouse at the time of death or be eligible for income benefits.

Taxation

Social Security income is not taxable unless your total taxable income (plus any tax-exempt interest, and 1/2 of your Social Security benefit) exceeds $25,000 in a given year if you are single ($32,000 combined income if married). If it does exceed that amount, then between 50% and 85% may be taxable depending on your overall income.

Reporting Requirement

If you are receiving benefits on behalf of children or other dependents, you will be asked via a letter from Social Security to report annually whether you spent or saved the money received for each child.

If you report that you saved any money, Social Security will ask for that money back when your child turns age 18, and will then turn around and send a check to your child for the same amount, whether or not you think that is in your child's best interests. Although not a requirement, Social Security also suggests that you "invest" all of the money into Federal Savings Bonds or Federal Deposit Insurance Corporation (FDIC) insured bank accounts, even though you may know of better options based on your child's situation.

Reporting that you spent all of each child's Social

Security income does not, of course, preclude you from saving money for your children if you so desire. If you want to save money for them, I suggest that you spend the Social Security and that you instead save other money (savings or income from any other sources - either DIC or SBP, or your personal income, savings, etc.). Doing so will give you greater flexibility and freedom to decide what is best for your own children, and reduce your reporting requirements.

It is my general recommendation that if the total amount received from Social Security is less than or equal to the total cost to take care of each child, that you report that you spent all of the Social Security money on each child's support, saving none.

As a parent, you are allowed to have your children's Social Security deposited into your checking account and use it for necessary expenses. But even if you have Social Security deposited into a separate account and let it build up for savings or some other reason, I would argue that on the annual report, you can still justify counting it as spent, up to the amount of the actual cost to care for your child(ren). It is "in one pocket and out the other," as some people say, meaning that you could reimburse yourself for your child's expenses at any time even if you choose not to do so.

Children

You should be eligible to receive a monthly Social Security income while under age 18 (or 19 if you are still in High School) or at any age if you are disabled and the disability started prior to age 22, assuming you were considered dependent on your parent for more than 50% of your support.

Your Surviving parent or guardian will receive your income and use it to take care of you until you turn age 18 (or older if you are disabled and considered unable to manage your finances). If you are 18 and still in high school, the Social Security will be paid directly to you, although you will be required to complete a certification of eligibility.

Lump Sums

If you are eligible for income benefits as a surviving child and there is no surviving spouse, you may be eligible to receive a one time lump sum death benefit of $255.

Also, if your surviving parent/guardian saved some of your monthly income benefit for you and informed the Social Security Administration accordingly, he/she will be required to pay it back to Social Security when you turn 18. Social Security will then pay the money directly to you.

Contact Social Security

You can reach Social Security at 800-772-1213 for enrollment or benefit questions or service. You can also create an account at ssa.gov/myaccount and view many important details. You can also find your nearest local office at ssa.gov/locator for in-person assistance.

Section Three

Lump Sum Benefits

Chapter Twelve

Servicemembers Group Life Insurance (SGLI)

Servicemembers Group Life Insurance (SGLI) is an optional group life insurance program for military Service Members, administered by the Prudential Life Insurance Company. Coverage is available in increments of $50,000, up to a maximum of $400,000 at a cost of seven cents per month per $1,000. Enrollment in the maximum coverage is automatic for a total of $28 per month, but Service Members may opt out or reduce coverage at their own election.

Recent Beneficiaries

If you are an SGLI beneficiary, you should generally expect to receive your proceeds within approximately three weeks of submitting your application, although I have seen it take as little as 11 days or as long as several months or more (typically due to complications with paperwork/beneficiary designations, etc.). You will receive taxable interest in addition to your tax-free lump sum amount, which accrues daily (currently at 0.5% annual percentage yield) until payment is issued.

You have the option to receive SGLI proceeds divided into 36 equal monthly installments based on the current interest rate (fixed for the three years). If your loved one pre-selected the 36-month payment option, however, you will not be able to change the election to receive a lump sum.

You may choose to receive your proceeds either via direct deposit, check, or what is called an Alliance account - a non-FDIC insured interest bearing account with Prudential (currently earning 0.5% annual interest) that includes a checkbook for easy withdrawals. I typically recommend choosing the Alliance account option if your checking/savings account earns less than 0.5% interest, although I recommend moving the money as soon as you are able to find an account that earns a higher rate of interest. There are many online and often some local options that pay more than 1% interest annually for savings/money market accounts. It may not sound like it is worth your time, but an extra 0.5% interest on $400,000 (if you received the full SGLI) is an extra $166.67 per month, and can often be set up in a matter of minutes.

Minor Beneficiaries

If there are beneficiaries who are minors, a court appointed conservator must generally be established prior to SGLI/Prudential releasing the funds. This may vary based on the state of residence and the amount of money that the beneficiary will receive (e.g. Colorado allows minors to have up to $10,000 in assets before requiring a conservator).

What to do with the Money

If you are a beneficiary of or have recently received SGLI you may wonder what you should do with the money. Even if years have passed, you may wonder if you did the right thing, or if you could have done better.

If this is your first opportunity to invest, the idea may seem overwhelming, so take your time and make sure that you feel comfortable with whatever decisions that you make. Focus first on balancing your budget (i.e. spend less than your income each month) and strive to save 10% or more of your current income to add to your investments. Doing so will provide you with a sense of control and confidence to make wise decisions, especially during difficult times.

Sometimes, the first "investment" you should make is to simply move most of your bank account balance to a new savings account that earns more interest, or perhaps into a savings account within a Roth Individual Retirement Arrangement (IRA) if eligible, so that the interest will accrue tax free/deferred.

HEART Act

The Heroes Earnings Assistance and Relief Tax (H.E.A.R.T.) Act of 2008 dictates that you may contribute ("roll over," as the IRS classifies it) up to 100% of SGLI or Death Gratuity proceeds that were paid as a result of "death from injury" into a Roth IRA or a Coverdell Education Savings Account (ESA). Both of these types of accounts have special tax benefits and other protections. However, you have only one year after receiving the money to make the contribution(s), because normally you can only contribute up to $5,500 per year into a Roth IRA (and only if you had earned income), or $2,000 per year into a Coverdell Savings Account.

Roth Individual Retirement Arrangements (Roth IRA's)

A Roth IRA is a uniquely special type of account with very favorable tax treatment. First, it is perhaps the only type of account that allows you to withdraw your contributions (basis/principle) at any time and at any age without incurring taxes or penalties, regardless of how much interest or other earnings you have gained within the account (or multiple accounts, if you have more than one). After withdrawing all of your principle, you can withdraw your earnings tax and penalty free at age 59 ½ (assuming you have owned a Roth IRA for at least five years at that point), or penalty free at any age if used for a regular income stream under section 72(t) distributions.

Other special penalty exceptions exist for withdrawals used for items such as qualified higher education expenses, disability-related expenses, the purchase of a first home (up to $10,000 lifetime if you have not owned a "main home" in the last two years), deductible medical expenses, unemployed health insurance, qualified Reservist distributions and IRS levies.

Additionally, Roth IRA accounts are protected from creditors or personal liability (up to certain limits) in many states, and Federally via bankruptcy laws, up to $1,283,025 as of April 1, 2016 (adjusts for inflation every three years).

You also do not have to report Roth IRA funds as assets on the Free Application for Federal Student Aid (FAFSA) and your family may therefore benefit from increased financial aid eligibility while attending college. However, be careful when making withdrawals from IRA's while you or your dependents attend college (or the two years before) because the FAFSA counts withdrawals as income even if they are really just a return of principal. The extra "income" may or may not have an actual affect on your financial aid depending on your overall situation, but should be planned for in advance if possible.

I rarely find a downside to contributing as much as possible to a Roth IRA. The tax savings alone could add up to tens of thousands or even hundreds of thousands or millions of dollars over your lifetime (and that of your children or other beneficiaries, if left to them properly).

Holding your assets in a Roth IRA can also prevent you from losing eligibility for the Earned Income Tax Credit (EITC) if you earn a modest income from working and you have children or other qualifying dependents (e.g. under $39,617 in wages in 2016 for single filers with one dependent). Interest, dividends, capital gains and other investment earnings of over $3,450 during a year ($3,500 in 2017) make you ineligible for the credit. Even $400,000 yielding 1% will earn you $4,000 a year in interest, which could literally cost you more in tax credits than the interest you earned (the maximum earned income tax credit for 2017 is $6,318). But earning that same $4,000 in interest within a Roth IRA would prevent you from losing the credit.

Investment Options

Nearly any type of savings or investment can be held inside of a Roth IRA, except for certain collectibles, life insurance policies and self-dealing assets (S-corporations, real estate that you live in, etc.). Common choices include savings accounts, CD's (Certificates of Deposit – time restricted savings that often pay higher rates of interest than savings accounts but charge a fee for withdrawing your money prior to specified a specified length of time), stocks (partial ownership in corporations), bonds (loans to governments or businesses for a specified length of time and rate of interest), mutual funds (pooled investments in stocks and/or bonds), exchange traded funds (pooled investments similar to mutual funds, but traded on stock exchanges), and annuities (hybrid insurance-investment/savings vehicles, often used to generate guaranteed lifetime income, although access to principal is often restricted or eliminated).

Many alternative investments, though generally considered higher risk, are also allowed within their Roth IRA's, subject to custodian (the financial firm/company that has custody of your assets) restrictions. Examples include, but are not limited to: privately held companies (subject to self-dealing rules), gold, silver, platinum or palladium bullion (subject to certain types, conditions and limitations), investment real estate (must be handled carefully and according to very specific rules and guidelines), etc.

Coverdell Education Savings Accounts (ESA's)

You have up to one year after receiving SGLI or DG proceeds (as a result of death from injury), to contribute up to the full amount you received to Coverdell ESA's (reduced by any contribution ("roll over") to Roth IRA's).

Coverdell ESA's are lesser known, lesser used accounts that uniquely allow you to avoid taxes on earnings that are used for not only higher education, but also elementary, middle and high school expenses of a beneficiary. In addition to tuition and fees, qualified withdrawals may be made from Coverdell ESA's to cover the cost of room and board, computers, software and even internet access.

Servicemembers Group Life Insurance Traumatic Injury Protection (TSGLI)

Most Service Members pay $1 per month for what is often referred to as Traumatic SGLI (TSGLI). TSGLI pays $25,000 to $100,000 in a tax-free lump sum as a result of certain severe injuries and hospitalizations while on active duty (combat or non-combat related) if the injured survives for at least seven days. Enrollment is automatic for Service Members who accept automatic enrollment in SGLI. Traumatic Brain Injuries (TBI), major facial injuries, virtually any hospitalization from injury of 15 days or more, loss of limbs, fingers, toes, etc. and temporary or permanent loss of hearing, vision, and other injuries will trigger a TSGLI claim eligibility.

If your loved one survived major injuries for seven days

or more, and he/she/you did not receive TSGLI proceeds, you may still apply to receive them, as they will generally be paid to the same beneficiary/beneficiaries who received SGLI.

Family SGLI (FSGLI)

Family SGLI (FSGLI) is a life insurance program available to Service Members to provide coverage for their spouse for up to $100,000 (available in $10,000 increments) and children for $10,000 per child if spouse coverage is elected (children are covered at no cost up to age 18, or 23 if a full-time student or any age if permanently disabled prior to turning age 18). The cost is currently 50 cents per $10,000 or $5 per month for maximum coverage for spouses under age 35 (premiums are higher for spouses age 35 and older). Enrollment in FSGLI is automatic for married Service Members whose spouse is not in the military, and can be applied for in the case of dual military spouses.

If you are a surviving spouse, you may elect to continue your FSGLI coverage by converting it to a permanent commercial policy (typically whole life), without the need for underwriting of your health status, within 120 days after your loss. Generally, this life insurance coverage is expensive compared to what you might obtain on the open market if you are in good health and do not have a family history of hereditary, life shortening conditions. But if you or your immediate family members have or have had major health conditions, this may be a great opportunity to maintain your life insurance coverage. The cost is based on your age and the selected coverage amount, and generally a standard health rating. 11 companies currently participate, and rates vary. For example, I recently obtained several $100,000 whole life quotes for a 29-year-old client, and they ranged from $93-$110 per month. One company offered a $100,000 Universal life policy for $45 per month or a hybrid Term/Universal policy for $37 per month.

FinancialPoint®

One incredible benefit that is included for all SGLI, FSGLI, TSGLI and even Veterans Group Life Insurance (VGLI) beneficiaries, regardless of Line of Duty or marital status, is lifetime financial planning services through a VA sponsored program called FinancialPoint®.

FinancialPoint® has a 24-hour call center staffed with knowledgeable financial counselors if you have general questions, or would like a basic financial plan mailed to you.

You also have access to a fully-licensed professional who can provide you with customized, unbiased assistance and guidance in nearly all things financial-related via FinancialPoint's network of privately contracted financial planners/counselors. Some of the advisors in the network even have special knowledge and experience regarding Military Survivor benefits and programs.

Unlike approximately 98% of "financial advisors" in the United States, FinancialPoint® contracted advisors generally do not earn commissions or kickbacks of any kind. Their main incentive is to help you as much as possible, and in as many ways as possible. Your information stays private and confidential between you and your planner, and is not shared with the VA or the military under normal circumstances. Your advisor truly works for you, yet the cost is paid on your behalf.

Please still be aware that contracted advisors have varied opinions about how finances and investments should be handled. They may also have varied experience or familiarity with Military Surviving Family Members and related programs and benefits. Some may also offer investment management services for a separate cost. So it is still important that you decide if you are comfortable working with a given counselor. Do not be afraid to request another counselor if the one assigned to you does not meet your needs or if you move and you prefer to start your financial plan over with a new advisor.

I have worked through this program for over six years and love it! It has given me great freedom and flexibility to help Surviving family members as much as I can, and it enables focusing on your needs. There has been little to no red tape preventing me from assisting, so I have been able to focus on doing what I love best – helping you special families!

Even partial beneficiaries are fully entitled to FinancialPoint® benefits, so no matter how many of you are listed as beneficiaries on a policy, you each have your own separate entitlement to lifetime financial counseling. If you were not the beneficiary but you are the parent or guardian of a beneficiary, we can also start helping you on their behalf. If you are a spouse, we can often also help your children in many ways as part of your overall financial plan.

Contact OSGLI or FinancialPoint®

You can reach the Office of Servicemembers Group Life Insurance (OSGLI) at 1-800-419-1473 for information or to obtain your claim number.

You can enroll with FinancialPoint® at 888-243-7351 or fcs@financialpoint.com. To work directly with me/my firm, please call 719-313-5815 or email eric@militarysurvivor.com.

Chapter Thirteen

Death Gratuity (DG)

The Department of Defense pays a one-time, tax free lump sum payment of $100,000 called Death Gratuity (DG) to designated beneficiaries of active-duty Service Members and those who are determined to have died of a "service-connected" condition within 120 days after separating from service. Payment is generally made within 72 hours to Survivors of active-duty Service Members, initiated by their last military command. Beneficiaries of Service Members who die from a service-connected condition during the 120 days after separating from service must apply for the Death Gratuity through the department of Veterans Affairs. It can take several months or more to be paid because the line of duty investigation must be completed before payment can be issued.

The Death Gratuity is taxpayer funded. It was previously only $12,000 and taxable, and did not allow for beneficiary designations. It was intended to assist dependent family members with immediate needs since military pay ceases immediately after a Service Member dies, while months may pass before VA DIC and/or SBP, Social Security, etc. begin.

If you were dependent on your loved one for financial support and were not selected as the DG beneficiary, Army Emergency Relief (AER), Navy-Marine Corps Relief Society (NMCRS), Coast Guard Mutual Assistance (CGMA) or the Air Force Aid Society (AFAS) may be able to grant a bridge loan or other assistance to help you with your immediate needs while you await the processing of your income and other lump sum payments.

Chapter Fourteen

Other Lump Sums

Unpaid pay/allowances

If you were the designated beneficiary for unpaid pay and allowances, you will receive a one time, taxable distribution equal to any unpaid pay, sick pay, vacation pay or other allowances that were due to your loved one at the time of his or her passing. Typically, the last paycheck will also be "frozen" and included in this amount. Occasionally a mistake occurs and the last paycheck is not frozen, in which case the Department of Defense (DOD) generally asks for the money back so it can turn around and reissue it to you, assuming you are the beneficiary.

BAH – Spouses and Children

You should receive 365 days of Base Allowance for

Housing (BAH) in a tax-free lump sum payment if your Service Member was on active duty. If you are living on a military installation, you generally have the option to stay in your housing for up to 365 days, although you will still receive BAH in a single lump sum and you will be expected to pay rent directly to the housing office (so please do not mistake it for spending money if you need it to pay the rent).

GI Bill Refund

If your Service Member paid into the Montgomery G.I. Bill (typically $100 per month for 12 months), you may be eligible to receive a refund of those payments (typically a total of $1,200). The refund is paid to the SGLI beneficiaries, or to the Surviving Spouse, Children or Parents (in that order) if SGLI was opted out of or no beneficiaries were named.

Social Security

As mentioned previously, Social Security pays a one-time $255 lump sum death benefit to Surviving Spouses who were living with their spouse at the time of death or who are eligible for income benefits based on his/her record. If there is no eligible Surviving Spouse, a Surviving Child may be eligible for the lump sum if eligible to receive Social Security Survivor income benefits.

Private Life Insurance

If you are the beneficiary of private life insurance, you should receive your proceeds tax-free, but the interest that you accrue will be taxable (interest accrues from day one up until the day payment is issued).

If you have not yet applied to receive your proceeds yet, the process is generally straightforward. You typically contact the company and notify them that you are a/the beneficiary of the policy. They will most likely ask you a few questions to verify your identity and your beneficiary status, and then have you fill out an application and provide documentation, including a civilian death certificate (they most often will not accept the military's DD1300). If they determine that you are not the beneficiary, they will not likely give you any further information.

Retained Asset Accounts

Most life insurance companies offer a type of holding account, sometimes referred to as "retained asset accounts," that often pay higher than average market rates of interest if you leave your money there, sometimes ranging as high as 3-4%. They typically come with a checkbook so that you can withdraw money at any time, although they may have a minimum withdrawal amount or a maximum amount of withdrawals/checks per years.

Retained asset accounts are not FDIC insured like most bank accounts, but instead are subject to the claims-paying ability of insurance companies. They are, however, protected by state guaranty associations (GA) which provide coverage to affected people in the case of an insurance company failure. The protection varies depending on your state of residence, but is generally around $300,000 per policy (multiple beneficiaries may reduce your coverage).

Insurance companies often consider retained asset accounts a "win-win" situation that allows them to retain some of the cash that they would have to pay out in insurance proceeds, while paying you a higher than market rate of interest for savings funds. They generally earn a "spread" over what they pay you, which is similar to what banks do with your deposits (e.g. they may be able to earn 4.5% interest on their bonds, while paying you 3%). They also retain the ability to offer you other highly profitable insurance, investment or annuity products.

Section Four

Other Benefits and Programs

Chapter Fifteen

Education

The Survivors' and Dependents' Educational Assistance (DEA) Chapter 35 VA Entitlement

Spouses

You are eligible for DEA if your spouse was determined to be "in the line of duty," "service connected" or had a total service-connected disability. It is a monthly income ($1,041 for full-time status as of October 1, 2017, prorated for part time attendance) paid directly to you while attending college or participating in other VA approved education programs (i.e. certain licenses, certifications, college entrance exam/etc.) for up to 45 full-time months (breaks excepted, so it is equivalent to five years of full time education). It may also be reduced if you are eligible for your own G.I. Bill entitlement or received a previously transferred entitlement from the Post 9/11 GI Bill.

You have up to 20 years to complete your education and use this benefit if your husband was on active duty or totally disabled within three years of discharge (otherwise 10 years). Remarriage prior to the age of 57 terminates eligibility (but it can be reinstated if your remarriage ends).

As of 2015, you have the option to relinquish your DEA eligibility in lieu of the Fry Scholarship (see later section for details) if your spouse died "in line of duty" while on active duty after September 10, 2001. Be careful in making this election, because it is irrevocable, but in many cases, will result in a greater benefit.

Children

You are eligible for DEA if your parent was determined to be "in line of duty," "service connected" or had a total service-connected disability." It is a monthly income ($1,041 for full-time status as of October 1, 2017, prorated for part time attendance) paid directly to you while attending college or participating in other VA approved education programs (i.e. certain licenses, certifications, college entrance exam/etc.) for up to 45 full-time months (breaks excepted, so it is equivalent to five years of full time education). It may also be reduced if you are eligible for your own G.I. Bill entitlement or received a previously transferred entitlement from the Post 9/11 GI Bill. You must use DEA during the ages of 18 to 26, although some exceptions may be possible for granting an extension up to age 31 (e.g., if you are in the service).

You have the option to relinquish your DEA eligibility in lieu of the Fry Scholarship (see the next section for details) if your parent died "in line of duty" while on active duty after August 1, 2011. Be careful in making this election, because it is irrevocable, but in many cases will result in a greater benefit.

If your parent died on active duty in the line of duty after September 10, 2001 but before August 1, 2011, you are eligible for both DEA and the Fry Scholarship for a total of up to 81 months of education benefits. If this applies to you and if you plan to attend college/etc. for more than 4 years, it may make sense to receive the DEA first since it has a shorter eligibility period. But it is important to take all factors into consideration when making a decision.

Machine Gunnery Sergeant John David Fry Scholarship

Spouses

The Fry Scholarship essentially entitles you to the Post 9/11 GI Bill if your spouse was on active duty and "in line of duty" and died after September 10, 2001. If you choose to use the Fry Scholarship benefit, however, you permanently lose eligibility for DEA entitlement, and you must make an irrevocable election upon accessing education benefits after

January 1, 2015. Recent legislation eliminated the time limit for you to use your Fry Scholarship, although remarriage will end your eligibility.

The Fry Scholarship pays 100% of in-state tuition and fees for public college and university attendance or up to $22,805.34 (as of August 1, 2017) per year for private school education for 36 months (excluding breaks, so it is up to four years of full time education). It is not eligible for the Yellow Ribbon program (a reduced tuition agreement that certain schools have with the VA). Other VA approved education programs (i.e. certain licenses, certifications, college entrance exam/etc.) are covered.

In addition, you will receive an annual book/Supplies Stipend of $1,000 (if attending full time) and a Monthly Housing Allowance (MHA) which in most cases is the equivalent of Basic Allowance for Housing (BAH) for an E-5 with dependents, based on the zip code of your school. If you are attending in a foreign country, MHA is $1,681 per month (as of August 1, 2017). If all of your classes are online, you will receive $840.50 per month. You can receive prorated tuition/books benefits and MHA for less than full-time attendance, but you must attend more than half-time to be eligible for any housing allowance (attending half time or less makes you completely ineligible for MHA).

In-state Tuition Classification

Effective July 1, 2017, all public colleges/universities must charge you the in-state tuition rate while using the Fry Scholarship, even if you would not otherwise qualify for in-state tuition. Effectively, this means that if you want to move to a new state and attend a public school, you will not have to pay the difference between in-state and out-of-state tuition (which you otherwise would have been responsible to pay).

Children

The Fry Scholarship essentially entitles you to the Post 9/11 GI Bill until age 33 if your parent was on active duty and "in line of duty" and died after September 10, 2001. If your parent died prior to August 1, 2011 you maintain eligibility for both DEA and Fry, but you may only use one at a time. If you choose to use the Fry Scholarship benefit and your parent died after July 31, 2011, you permanently lose eligibility for DEA, and you must make an irrevocable election upon application.

The Fry Scholarship pays 100% of in-state tuition and fees for public college and university attendance or up to $22,805.34 (as of August 1, 2017) per year for private school education for 36 months (excluding breaks, so it is up to four years of full time education). It is not eligible for the Yellow Ribbon program (a reduced tuition agreement that certain schools have with the VA). Other VA approved education programs (i.e. certain licenses, certifications, college entrance exam/etc.) are covered.

In addition, you will receive an annual book/Supplies Stipend of $1,000 (if attending full time) and a Monthly Housing Allowance (MHA) which in most cases is the equivalent of Basic Allowance for Housing (BAH) for an E-5 with dependents, based on the zip code of your school. If you are attending in a foreign country, MHA is $1,681 per month (as of August 1, 2017). If all of your classes are online, you will receive $840.50 per month. You can receive prorated tuition/books benefits and MHA for less than full-time attendance, but you must attend more than half-time to be eligible for any housing allowance (attending half time or less makes you completely ineligible for MHA).

In-state Tuition Classification

Effective July 1, 2017, all public colleges/universities must charge you the in-state tuition rate while using the Fry Scholarship, even if you would not otherwise qualify for in-state tuition. Effectively, this means that if you want to move to a new state and attend a public school, you will not have to pay the difference between in-state and out-of-state tuition (which you otherwise would have been responsible to pay).

Scholarships and other Financial Aid

Many other organizations interested in assisting Military Surviving Spouses and Children with education costs have raised a substantial amount of money to do so, and may even assist with computers and supplies, room and board, etc. even if all of your other educational expenses are already covered by the VA/other aid. Some programs have recently even started assisting with student loan repayment for children who have received their bachelor's degree.

Other financial aid may be available depending on your degree choice, grade point average, extracurricular activities, school club involvement, demographic characteristics (such as heritage, race, gender, family history, etc.), hobbies, career pursuits, etc.

If you would like us to provide you with a customized scholarship list that applies to your specific circumstances, and/or if you would like us to help you with applying for/obtaining any of aid/scholarships offered, please contact us via www.militarysurvivor.com or call 719-313-5815 or email me at eric@militarysurvivor.com.

Chapter Sixteen

Medical Care

Spouses

If your spouse was on active duty status for more than 30 consecutive days at the time of passing, you are eligible to receive the equivalent of active-duty health care coverage for up to three years and then retiree coverage for life (or until remarriage, which permanently ends eligibility even if the remarriage ends (unless it is annulled)).

If your spouse was on active-duty status for 30 days or less, you are not eligible for the three years of active-duty equivalent health care coverage, but you are immediately eligible for retiree coverage.

If your spouse was in the National Guard or Reserves but not activated or on duty (including monthly weekend duty and annual training), you may be eligible to purchase TRICARE Reserve Select (TRS) coverage for up to six months, at a rate of $47.82 for individuals and $217.51 per month for family coverage (changing to $46.09 and $221.38 respectively on January 1, 2018).

The Active Duty version of TRICARE Prime requires no premium and generally nominal or no copays. However, if you obtain non-emergency care without a referral from your primary care manager (PCM), you will incur point-of-service charges equivalent to 50% of the incurred charges after a $300 deductible, plus any extra charges from using nonparticipating providers (if applicable).

The retiree version of TRICARE Prime currently requires an annual payment of $282.60 for individuals (although your premium will be "frozen" or fixed at the rate that it was at the time that you became a Survivor, so long as you have continuously resided in the United States and you or any of your family members have continuously been enrolled in TRICARE Prime). It also requires increased copays depending on the type of medical services received (e.g. $20 for ambulance, $30 for emergency room, $11 per day for hospitalization, etc.). If you are transitioning from three years of active-duty Tricare Prime coverage to the retiree plan, you must re-enroll or you will be automatically switch TRICARE Standard and Extra.

TRICARE Standard and Extra offers more flexibility with

your health care if you do not mind paying more by way of cost-sharing and copays. TRICARE Standard refers to the use of non-network providers, while TRICARE Extra is the term that applies when you use in-network providers. No primary care manager (PCM) is required, and therefore no referral is required for you to obtain necessary medical care (although some procedures require pre-authorization).

As with TRICARE Prime, during the first three years if you are eligible you receive the active-duty version of TRICARE Standard and Extra. This means a $150 deductible per fiscal year (October 1 to September 30), 15% cost sharing for in-network providers (and/or nominal copays, such as $25 for ambulance, $17.80 per day for hospitalization) and 20% cost-sharing for nonparticipating providers, up to an out of pocket maximum (the "catastrophic cap" or maximum you are personally required to contribute toward your health care per year, including deductible, copays and cost-sharing) of only $1,000 per fiscal year. If you use non-network providers, however, you are responsible for any charges that exceed the allowable amount that in-network providers can charge for the same services (generally limited to 15% extra for approved providers).

After three years, you will revert to the retiree plan. The annual deductible remains at $150, but cost sharing is increased to 20% for in-network and 25% for nonparticipating providers;

copays are also increased (e.g. $250 per day for hospitalization) or subject to the applicable cost-sharing percentage, and the annual maximum out-of-pocket increases to $3,000 per year.

To enroll in TRICARE Standard and Extra, you must simply dis-enroll from TRICARE Prime. Keep in mind that you may be restricted from re-enrolling in TRICARE Prime for up to one year.

Children

Surviving dependent children (or other dependents enrolled in DEERS receiving at least 50% of their support from the Service Member) of active-duty Service Members that were on active duty for more than 30 consecutive days receive active-duty health care coverage until age 21 (unless marriage or other disqualifying event occurs) or age 23 if enrolled full-time in an approved program of higher education.

You are therefore eligible for TRICARE Prime at no cost and generally with no copays as long as you remain eligible. If while covered under TRICARE Prime, however, you get non-emergency care without a referral from your primary care manager (PCM), you incur point-of-service charges equivalent to 50% of the incurred charges after a $300 deductible, plus any extra charges if using nonparticipating providers (generally up to 15% of normal TRICARE charges if services provided within the U.S.).

Alternatively, you have the option to dis-enroll from TRICARE Prime and therefore become covered by TRICARE Standard and Extra. With TRICARE Standard and Extra, no primary care manager (PCM) is required, and therefore no referral is required for you to obtain necessary medical care (although some procedures require pre-authorization).

TRICARE Extra is the term that applies when you use in-network providers, and TRICARE Standard refers to the use of non-network providers.

Under TRICARE Standard and Extra, you will be responsible to pay a $150 deductible per fiscal year (October 1 to September 30), 15% cost-sharing for in-network providers (and/or nominal copays, such as $25 for ambulance, $17.80 per day for hospitalization) and 20% cost-sharing for nonparticipating providers, up to an out of pocket maximum (the "catastrophic cap" or maximum you are personally required to contribute toward your health care per year, including deductible, copays and cost-sharing) of $1,000 per fiscal year. If you use non-network providers, you are also responsible for any charges that exceed the allowable amount that in-network providers can charge for the same services (generally limited to 15% extra for approved providers).

Keep in mind that if you dis-enroll from TRICARE Prime, you may be restricted from re-enrolling for up to one year.

If your parent's active-duty status was than 30 days or less, retiree benefits and costs apply, and the duration of eligibility is the same.

The retiree version of TRICARE Prime currently requires an annual payment of $282.60 per person or $565.20 per family (although your premium will be "frozen" or fixed at the rate that it was at the time that you became a Survivor, so long as you have continuously resided in the United States and you or any of your family members have continuously been enrolled in TRICARE Prime). It also requires nominal copays depending on the type of medical services received (e.g. $20 for ambulance, $30 for emergency room, $11 per day for hospitalization, etc.).

The retiree version of TRICARE Standard and Extra can be selected by dis-enrolling from TRICARE Prime. It carries an annual deductible of $150, cost sharing of 20% for in-network and 25% for non-network providers, copays for certain services (e.g. $250 per day for hospitalization), and is subject to an annual maximum out-of-pocket ("catastrophic cap") of $3,000 per fiscal year.

Children of Reserve or National Guard Service Members who were not in the line of duty at the time of their passing are eligible for TRICARE Reserve Select for up to six months. Enrollment is automatic if coverage was in effect, and costs $46.09 for individuals and $221.38 for families, effective January 1, 2018.

Tricare Young Adult

You are eligible to continue Tricare coverage after age 21 (or 23 if in school) until age 26 by enrolling in TRICARE Young Adult (TYA) Prime or Standard (as long as you are not married and are not eligible for health care coverage under your own employer sponsored plan). As of January 1, 2017, monthly premiums of $319 are required to maintain coverage in TYA Prime, and $216 for TYA Standard. Coverages, copays and cost-sharing amounts are the same as the active-duty or retiree version in which you were previously enrolled.

Based on the new premium structure, I see no mathematical way in which TYA Prime is better than standard for surviving children of active-duty Service Members unless you are in a very high tax bracket, because the maximum out of pocket costs for TYA Standard is only $1,000 but the extra premiums for TYA Prime is $1,236.

You may dis-enroll at any time from TYA, but you will be blocked from re-enrolling for 12 months unless you dis-enrolled because you became eligible for your own employer-sponsored healthcare plan (and are no longer eligible for it).

Other Options

Keep in mind that other options for healthcare may be less expensive than Tricare Young Adult, for similar or broader coverage. For example, you may be eligible for Medicaid or for an Affordable Care Act Subsidy depending on your overall situation (income, assets, the state you live in, marital status, children, household income, etc.) and depending on how much medical care you need. Health sharing "ministries" also exist that are similar to insurance and exempt you from Obamacare penalties, and may cost as little as $45 per month.

Parents

Parents or parents-in-law who were financial dependents of their Service Member may be eligible for TRICARE Plus, which is a space available program offered only on participating military installations, and covers only primary care (no specialty care) at no cost.

Chapter Seventeen

Dental Care

Spouses

Surviving Spouses of Active-duty Service Members and members of the Selected Reserve of the Ready Reserve and Individual Ready Reserve (regardless of whether they were activated at the time) are eligible for premium free dental coverage through the TRICARE Dental Program (TDP) for up to three years, after which eligibility continues through the TRICARE Retiree Dental Program (only if your spouse was on active duty for more than 30 days).

Under the TRICARE Dental Program, diagnostic and preventative services are generally covered with no out of pocket cost to you, and most other services are covered with cost-sharing ranging from 20-50% with an annual maximum benefit of $1,500 (May 1 to April 30). There is an additional $1,200 maximum for accident-related dental work. Orthodontia has a separate lifetime maximum of $1,750.

Under the TRICARE Retiree Dental Program (TRDP), monthly premiums of approximately $25-$40 (based on zip code of your residence) are required. There is also a $50 annual deductible and a one year waiting period for certain procedures (unless you enroll within four months of becoming eligible, and request a waiver of the waiting period). The annual maximum benefit is $1,300, plus $1,200 for accident-related work and a lifetime orthodontia maximum of $1,750.

Children

Dependent children (or other dependents enrolled in DEERS) of active-duty status Service Members as well as members of the Selected Reserve of the Ready Reserve and Individual Ready Reserve (regardless of whether they were activated at the time) are eligible for premium free dental coverage through the TRICARE Dental Program (TDP) until age 21 (unless marriage or other disqualifying event occurs) or age 23 if enrolled full time in an approved education program.

Under the TRICARE Dental Program, diagnostic and preventative services are generally covered with no out of pocket cost to you, and most other services are covered with cost-sharing ranging from 20-50% with an annual maximum benefit of $1,500 (May 1 to April 30). There is an additional $1,200 maximum for accident-related dental work. Orthodontia has a separate lifetime maximum of $1,750.

Chapter Eighteen

Other Benefits and Programs

Final Move

Joint Personal Property Shipping Office (JPPSO) will generally provide spouses and dependents of active-duty Service Members with a no cost move within three years of the death of their sponsor. If you are not planning to move during the first three years but you think you might move soon thereafter, you can apply for an extension. I have observed extensions granted for up to several additional years depending on the circumstances.

Homeowners Assistance Program (HAP)

If your Service Member died in a combat zone or became terminally ill or mortally wounded there, and you own a home and are interested in moving during the subsequent two years, the Homeowners Assistance Program (HAP) will either buy your house from you, pay off your mortgage balance (in exchange for the deed) or reimburse you for up to 95 percent of the purchase price of your home. It will also pay for your closing costs (including real estate agent fees and other typical and customary closing costs, including a limited credit toward buyer closing costs).

HAP is of particular benefit if your house is worth close to or less than what you paid for it or owe on it, but is a great benefit even if you sell it for a profit, as it will pay up to tens of thousands of dollars in closing costs.

If you are coming up on the two-year mark and you are interested in selling your home but are not quite ready, you should apply before the deadline as in many cases an extension may be granted and/or the program administrators will give you time to get the house ready to sell and get it listed and actually sold.

Private Organizations

A great number of private organizations and nonprofits have been created by caring individuals who seek to honor your family's service and sacrifices for our country by providing you with anything from financial grants to scholarships to memorial-type items including quilts, portraits, paintings etc., getaways/trips, emotional support/counseling, etc. Due to the fact that their requirements vary and services/support offerings constantly change, I hope to keep an up to date list at www.militarysurvivor.com. Please check to see which ones you may be eligible for / interested in, and also inform us of anything that we do not have listed so that we can maintain a constantly updated, accurate and complete list.

A few quick examples:

Snowball Express®

Snowball Express provides an all-expenses-paid annual trip and events for children ages 5-18 of deceased active-duty Service Members, and a guardian. Surviving family members enjoy special charter airline flights, police escorts to special events, fun activities, meals and other events to honor and remember your fallen hero(es). Thousands of Military Surviving Family Members from across the globe attend this special trip each year, which generally takes place during the second week in December in the Dallas-Fort Worth area.

Chase® Bank Debt Cancellation

Chase Bank has a Military Survivor Program that cancels "mortgages, auto loans, credit cards, student loans and other consumer and business debt" for Service Members "killed in combat action or died in a combat theater of operations since January 1, 2011," including part or all of joint debt, subject to certain limitations. Be aware that some or all of the cancelled debt may become taxable income reportable on your income tax return. If your loved one had debt with Chase and you were unaware of this program and paid off all or part of the debt, you may still have your payments refunded to you.

Personalized Report

If you would like us to provide you with a customized list of private programs and benefits that apply to your specific circumstances, and/or if you would like us to help you with applying for/obtaining any of the services/support offered, please contact us via www.militarysurvivor.com or call 719-313-5815 or email me at eric@militarysurvivor.com.

Section Five

Other Financial Topics

Chapter Nineteen

Taxes

I have done my best to cover tax topics throughout the book as it applies to each section, but I will also include a basic summary of some important tax items and a few general rules and items of interest to be aware of.

What is taxable?

Anything received from the VA is not taxable, including monthly income benefits (e.g. DIC), education benefits, etc.

SGLI and Death Gratuity proceeds, private life insurance proceeds, and BAH lump sums are generally not taxable, although any interest associated with them will be taxable.

Unpaid pay and allowances is a lump sum payment that is taxable to the recipient.

SBP is taxable and often triggers a filing requirement and taxes due, even if paid to children.

Social Security is up to 85% taxable only to individuals that have taxable income over $25,000 (including one half of income received from Social Security) or couples earning over $32,000.

Dependency Status of Children receiving income

A fairly unique scenario applies to children who receive SBP and/or Social Security income. For dependency purposes, the IRS generally considers both incomes as provided by the children (as illogical as that may seem). So in many cases the children would not be considered a dependent if the benefits add up to more than half of their support. However, this does not exclude you from claiming them as qualifying children with regard to the earned income credit if they lived with you for more than half the year and you had earned income from working.

If you did not have income from working and/or did not have taxable income overall, not claiming your children as dependents may actually be financially beneficial, especially if each child's overall taxable income also remains low.

Alternative Minimum Tax (AMT) for children

When a child is the sole recipient of SBP, taxes may rise higher than expected due to an unfortunate tax law written into Alternative Minimum Tax (AMT) legislation. The AMT applies to all unearned income to minors that exceeds $7,400 ($7,450 in 2017) at a rate of 26%. I believe that the law was created to prevent wealthy adults from transferring assets to a child's name to avoid income taxes, but an unintended consequence of this law is that military surviving children are often laden with the tax.

I hope that Congress will pass an exemption to this law to SBP beneficiaries, but to my knowledge, nothing has been acted upon or is under consideration at this time. My understanding is that the Gold Star Wives have it on their list of potential legislations to advocate, but I am not sure how high of a priority it is.

Tax Refunds for Service Members Killed in Action

If your loved one was killed in action or died as a result of wounds or illnesses incurred while in a combat zone, you should be eligible to apply for a refund/exemption from all taxes paid/owed back to the year of first deployment to a combat zone. This includes any amounts withheld from wages from any job, taxes and penalties on retirement plan distributions, etc. All taxes are forgiven and refunded.

I have witnessed these refunds add up to thousands or even tens of thousands of dollars in some cases, so it is definitely worth reviewing your returns and filing the necessary amendments if a refund may be due. I have had a few clients whose spouse was deployed to the Gulf War in 1991, and later died in Iraq or Afghanistan. We have been able to amend tax returns to apply for refunds for all tax years starting in 1991, so up to 20 years or more in some instances! The IRS also pays compound interest on the refunds, so for some years, the interest has been more than the base amount of the refund!

If you did not know about this law and have not applied, you may still be eligible to apply for it. In my experience, the IRS has interpreted the legislation as eliminating the normal statute of limitations on applying for and receiving refunds. Several of my clients have applied for refunds more than 10 years after the death of their loved one, and have still received the refunds, with interest (although I am not guaranteeing that the IRS will always interpret this law so favorably)!

If you feel like you may be eligible for these tax refunds

and would like us to help you to file amendments, please feel reach out to me for assistance.

Gift Taxes

If you gave or plan to give more than $15,000 during a single calendar year to any individual in 2018 ($14,000 or lower thresholds apply to earlier years), you are generally required to file a gift tax return (IRS form 709), which is due at the same time as your income tax return. You may claim the use of a lifetime gifting exemption of up to $5.49 million in 2017 ($5.6 million in 2018, lower thresholds apply to earlier years) to avoid owing any taxes. But you must file a gift tax return to do so. Otherwise you could owe taxes of 18-40% depending on the amount given (no taxes are generally due to recipients of gifts although the IRS may have power to collect from them from recipients if givers fail to pay).

If you have ever given more than the annual exclusion amount and did not know that you needed to file a gift tax return or failed to file for any other reason, it is likely not too late to do so. Assuming that you are able to claim an exemption and will not owe any taxes, there should be no penalty for filing. It is also my understanding that it is only too late to file if you have received a deficiency notice from the IRS due to a discovery of gifts that you made. But if you are proactive and file for past years without having received a notice from the IRS, you should be okay.

Chapter Twenty
Other Planning Topics

Buying a House

In the midst of the emotional excitement of buying a house, please take a moment to consider how easily you might be able to sell the house for the price you are paying if you had to unexpectedly move. You may not foresee any reason to move in the near future, but too often I have had clients who changed their minds or were compelled to move by other life circumstances sooner than they expected, and had no choice except to sell it for a loss or to become a landlord.

Especially if you are having a new home built in a neighborhood where many houses are still being built, it may be very difficult to sell your house without losing money for two to five or even ten years (after factoring in closing costs and potential real estate commissions, etc.). In a strong rising real estate market, you may not have a problem, but I encourage you to at least understand the potential costs of unexpectedly needing or wanting to move.

If you are already in the situation of wanting/needing to move while owning a home that you cannot sell for the amount you paid, and you are concerned about selling the house for a loss, ask yourself:

"Is your current house likely to go up in value faster than the house that you would like to purchase?"

If not, I think you should consider selling the house you are living in and move to where you would like to live (assuming you are getting a better value on the new house). I know it is hard to take a loss on anything, but if you do not sell and move, you are losing the increase in value of the house that you want to live in, which could make up for the loss on the house that you would like to sell. Purchase the house you want, and wait for *it* to go up in value.

Rent vs. Sell Your Home

If you want/need to move and you are in a difficult housing market or otherwise cannot sell your house for what you need/want to get out of it, you may consider it easier or more convenient or beneficial to rent it out instead of selling it.

In over a decade of being a landlord, I experienced good times and bad (very bad), so I want you to be aware of the many potential risks and rewards of renting out your house.

To decide if you are a good candidate for land-lordship, ask yourself:

"Am I interested in starting a rental property business?"

"If I did not currently own this specific property, would I consider purchasing it with the intent to rent it out?"

If the answer is "no," which it most often is, then I would strongly caution you to consider your other options more closely. Owning a rental property is a business, and it must be run like a business to have a good chance of success. Most renters do not treat houses with the care that the typical homeowner would, so you may find yourself responsible for costly repairs or other stresses that you would prefer not to deal with.

On the other hand, if you have been dreaming of being a landlord and the house you are living in is an ideal candidate, converting your home to a rental may have some advantageous tax benefits if you sell it within three years of moving out (if you have been living in it for at least two years). You may also have a lower interest rate on your mortgage than you could obtain if you were purchasing a house as an investment.

Advice from Other Military Survivors

Please send me feedback and other suggestions for your fellow Survivors to include in future editions / add to the website. eric@militarysurvivor.com

Most private pharmacies accept TRICARE, and often the cost is as little as $3 to fill a prescription. So, if your nearest military installation pharmacy has long lines and/or is not convenient, it might be worth your while to consider a local pharmacy. Also, for long term prescriptions, you can have them mailed to you via eScripts, typically at no cost.

-C. Sizer

Appendix

What Matters Most
Planning Activity

1. Name any <u>thing</u> that you have that you would not like to lose:
One minute time limit - assume that you will lose everything that you do not include here!

2. Name any <u>thing</u> that you would like to have (that you do not have):
One minute time limit - assume that you will have everything that you include here!

3. Name anyone that is important to you (past or present; also include pets):
One minute time limit, assume you will lose contact with / memory of anyone not included in this list!

4. Name any person or type of person that you hope will come into your life / become more important in your life:
One minute time limit - assume that anyone you list here will become a (greater) part of your life!

5. Name characteristics or values that you admire (or would like to further develop):
One minute time limit - assume that you will have/keep any characteristic or value included here!

6. Name any religious or spiritual beliefs or practices that you would like to maintain (or enhance):
One minute time limit - assume that you will keep/develop any belief or practice included here!

7. Name any desires, goals or achievements that you hope to accomplish during your lifetime:
One minute time limit – assume that you will fail at everything not listed here!

Now go back and circle anything that could be improved on and add an action plan of what it would take to accomplish your desired results.